WHSMITHS

Mary Norwak

WHSMITHS
FREEZER BOOK
Mary Norwak

this edition produced exclusively for
WHSMITH

Text filmset in Ehrhardt
Printed and bound by Toppan Printing Co.
Singapore

ACKNOWLEDGMENTS

The Publishers and Author want to thank the
following who have helped with photographs or
information for this book: Alcan Polyfoil Ltd;
Angel Studio; Bejam Bulk Buying Ltd; Birds
Eye Foods Ltd; British Bacon Curers'
Federation; British Meat Service; British
Sugar Bureau; H. P. Bulmer Ltd; Food
Advisory Service, Cadbury-Typhoo Ltd;
Cherry Valley Farms Ltd; Danish Agricultural
Producers; John Dixon; Dutch Dairy Bureau;
Electrolux Ltd; Flour Advisory Bureau;
Frigicold Ltd; Frozen Food Committee;
Mrs Julia Hedgcoe; G. E. C. (Domestic
Appliances) Ltd; Kellogg Company of Great
Britain Ltd; Lea and Perrins Ltd; New
Zealand Lamb Information Bureau; Oxo Ltd;
Philips Electrical Ltd; R. H. M. Foods Ltd;
Tabasco Sauce (Horlicks) Ltd; Walls (Ice
Cream) Ltd; Young's Seafoods Ltd.

CONTENTS

WEIGHTS AND MEASURES

Standard British weights and
measures are used throughout
the book. The following tables
give a simple conversions to
metric measures:

Weight	
1 oz =	28.35 grams
4 oz =	113.4 grams
8 oz =	226.8 grams
1 lb =	453.6 grams
	(0.45 kg)

Liquid Capacity	
1 fl oz	= 2.8 cl
¼ pt	= 14.2 cl
½ pt	= 28.35 cl
1 pt	= 56.7 cl
1 quart =	1.13 litres

Spoons	
1 teaspoon = 5 ml spoon
1 dessertspoon = 10 ml spoon
1 tablespoon = 15 ml spoon

Sugar boiling temperatures		
Soft ball	237°F	114°C
Hard ball	247°F	119°C
Soft crack	280°F	140°C
Hard crack	310°F	154°C
Caramel	340°F	171°C

Domestic oven temperatures

	Electric °F	Celsius °C	Gas
Very cool	225	110	¼
Very cool	250	130	½
Very cool	275	140	1
Cool	300	150	2
Warm	325	170	3
Moderate	350	180	4
Fairly hot	375	190	5
Fairly hot	400	200	6
Hot	425	220	7
Very hot	450	230	8
Very hot	475	240	9

Deep fat frying temperatures

Food	Bread browns in	Fat temperature	Oil temperature
Raw starchy foods doughnuts, fritters, chips (1st frying)	1¼ minutes	325°-340°F 170°C	340°F 170°C
Fish in batter	1¼ minutes	325°-340°F 170°C	340°F 170°C
Fish in egg and crumbs	1 minute	360°F 185°C	360°F 185°C
Scotch eggs	1 minute	350°F 180°C	350°F 180°C
Reheated foods potato straws, chips (2nd frying)	40 seconds	380°F 190°C	390°F 195°C

6

INTRODUCTION

Freezing is a quick method of preserving food safely. The activities of micro-organisms are slowed down as food approaches freezing point, and they become dormant at $0°$ F ($-18°$ C). Most home freezers are designed to bring the food down to this temperature, and to maintain it for storage. Some home freezers can have their temperature reduced by a further $5°$ to $10°$ F for fast freezing. But really deep freezing is only possible commercially; commercial frozen-food stores are usually maintained at $-20°$ F ($-29°$ C).

The advantages of home freezing and bulk buying are now appreciated by more and more people, both town and country dwellers. Not only does a home-freezing system save you money through economic purchasing of seasonal or commercially frozen raw materials, but you also save time in shopping and by using a system of batch cookery.

Your home freezer can serve a dual purpose. It can combine the long-term storage of bulk raw materials which you have frozen at home or have bought, and the short-term storage of fresh foods, cooked dishes and leftovers which will have a quick turnover.

As for a fridge, every housewife knows the value of this piece of equipment in our busy modern age, when both delivery services and personal shopping time are limited. It is the most vital piece of kitchen equipment one can have, after a cooker.

Cooked dishes for parties can be frozen when fresh foods are plentiful, and you can add the finishing touches just before serving.

8

YOUR FREEZER

ADAPTABLE FREEZING

Long-term storage is effective for the foods which you may buy cheaply from bulk suppliers; for farm and garden produce, and gluts of fresh food which are in season; also for special items, such as tropical fruits or rich cream, which you may get when on holiday, or which kind friends send you.

Short-term storage is a wonderful money-saver and way of varying meals by using cooked foods or leftovers. It is also useful if you do batch cookery of basic items such as roux or simple sauces: for items such as bread which you need regularly; you can buy them weekly or monthly: and for complete meals for sudden entertaining or emergency use.

Freezing is an easy process if you follow the basic instructions. These are not rigid rules but guide lines, showing how food can be kept well and retain flavour, colour and nutritive value. This book is designed for quick reference when preserving both raw materials and cooked foods. Types of food suitable for freezing are defined; but your individual requirements can only be assessed by experience, and by testing your favourite recipes under freezing conditions. The basic recipes included here are those which have proved successful in freezer storage and in subsequent cooking and eating.

The refrigerator is an invaluable aid to successful freezing. The freezer will function better if food is chilled in the refrigerator before being placed in the cabinet for freezing. The ice-making compartment of your refrigerator can also supply reserves of ice for rapidly chilling blanched vegetables and cooked dishes. Again, you can store large quantities of food temporarily in the refrigerator while the smaller recommended quantities are being frozen.

The refrigerator ice-making compartment can also be used for short-term storage of ice cream and other frozen products (see 'The Star System'). Frozen food should never be thawed quickly as rapid deterioration sets in, so the refrigerator is recommended for thawing almost all the items you freeze. The housewife who can assess her daily needs can transfer items from freezer to refrigerator storage first thing in the morning ready for later serving and further cooking if necessary.

The Star System

Frozen-food compartments on most British refrigerators are marked with stars in accordance with British Standards Specification No. 3739. This indicates recommended storage times for individual packets of commercially frozen foods.

* (one star) $-6°$ C or $21°$ F stores bought frozen food for one week, and ice cream for one day.

** (two star) $-12°$ C or $10°$ F stores bought frozen food for one month, and ice cream for two weeks.

*** (three star) $-18°$ C or $0°$ F stores bought frozen food for three months, and ice cream for one month.

Three-star frozen-food compartments are normally capable of freezing down to $0°$ F within 24 hours small quantities of fresh or cooked food, according to individual refrigerator manufacturers' instructions.

A true food freezer however is capable of always operating at $0°$ F ($-18°$ C) and is additionally capable of freezing unfrozen food to this temperature without any significant change in the temperature of the food already being stored. It can also store food for many months or even a year rather than weeks.

Four Star Marking

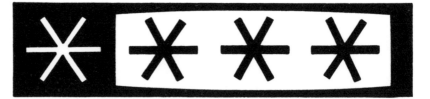

This symbol, consisting of a rectangular frame containing a large six-pointed star, and three small six-pointed stars in a curved frame distinguishes a true freezer compartment from the type above. The large star symbolises the food freezing capacity, and the three smaller stars (as used on frozen food storage compartments) indicate that most commercially-frozen foods can be stored up to three months. Manufacturers using this symbol must indicate in their instructions the maximum weight of food which can be frozen in 24 hours.

Running Costs

A freezer is not expensive to run. In average use, a 6 cubic food freezer uses .3 kW per cubic foot per 24 hours; 12 cubic foot uses .25 kW per cubic foot per 24 hours; 18 cubic foot uses .2 kW per 24 hours. The size of machine and its design, the frequency and length of time of opening, and the temperature of food to be frozen can affect running costs.

Insurance of Contents

The contents of a freezer can be valuable, particularly if large quantities of meat or game are stored. Only a small premium is usually required.

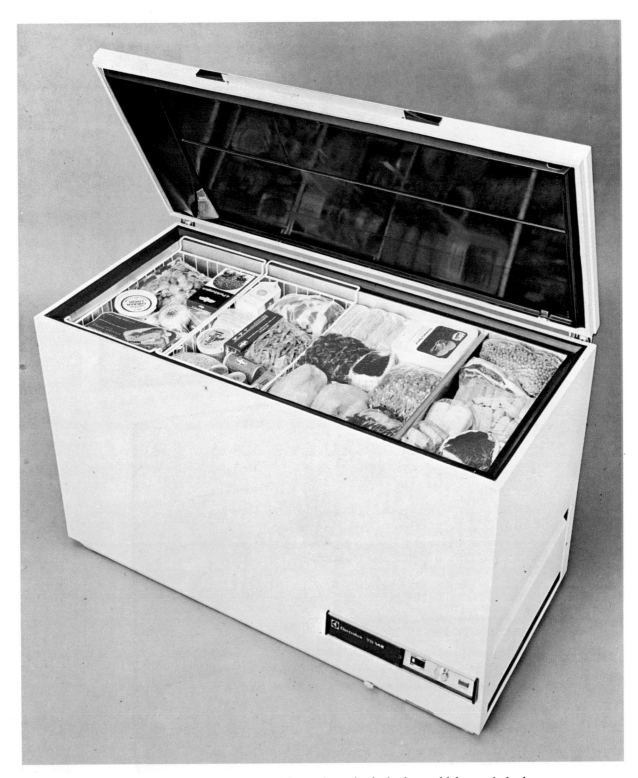

A chest freezer. Note the compact arrangement of the packages in the baskets, which contain both commercially frozen products and home-frozen produce.

A combination refrigerator freezer with equal-sized compartments, easy to use for slow thawing.

CHOOSING A FREEZER

The choice of a freezer will depend not only on the size of your family and the amount of your home produce but on the space available in kitchen or outhouse. Ideally, the freezer should be within easy reach of the cook, but excessive kitchen heat will put a heavy load on the cooling mechanism. Air must circulate freely round the freezer so that heat can be efficiently removed from the condenser. Dampness will damage both cabinet and motor.

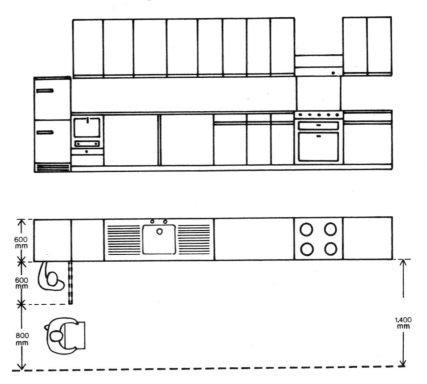

Site the freezer clear of the wall, well away from a cooker or fire.

Chest freezers are particularly suitable for locating in a garage or outhouse, and are excellent for bulk storage of such items as meat. Storage baskets make for tidiness, and help to divide food to be used soon from that which is kept for long-term storage. Very large commercial sizes are usually designed as chests, and can represent considerable economy in purchasing. It is important that a chest freezer has a magnetic lid seal and a self-balancing lid.

Upright freezers are very convenient for packing, with separate shelves for different types of food. There may be some slight intermittent rise in temperature in upright freezers as doors are often left open. Upright freezers have their weight concentrated in a small area, and it is important to check that the floor will take the weight of the freezer chosen.

Combination refrigerator freezers are very useful when space is limited as in a town house or flat. Normally, the freezer is on top of the refrigerator, but sometimes they are side by side. In either case the compartments are independent.

Special Features to look for

Most freezers have a light which comes on when the electricity supply is connected and

This close-up shows clearly the handles which support a top tier of hanging baskets. They are also used for lifting the baskets from here or from the freezer floor.

switched on; failure of the light means the power supply has been cut off and immediate investigation is necessary. Some freezers have a signal light connected to the thermostat which stays on as long as the cabinet temperature does not rise above a few degrees from the normal operating temperature.

Fast freezing compartments, switches and indicator lights are useful adjuncts to a freezer. Some freezers have a compartment divided by a panel or grid to keep still-unfrozen foods separate from stored foods while they are being processed. Some upright freezers have a shelf for fast freezing which is very useful for processing vegetables, cakes and pies which can be frozen before wrapping. The fast-freezing switch cuts out thermostatic control so that the motor runs continuously; heat is thus removed from unfrozen food as quickly as possible and the stored foods do not rise in temperature. The switch must be returned to normal running as soon as possible; sometimes the switch is wired in conjunction with an indicator light to show when the motor is running continuously.

Other useful additions to a freezer are storage baskets, which aid tidiness. Locks are useful to avoid pilfering if the freezer is stored in an outhouse; they also prevent children opening the freezer and leaving it open.

Installing the Freezer

A newly installed freezer should be washed inside with warm water and dried thoroughly, then set at the recommended temperature for everyday use. The cabinet should be chilled for 12 hours before use.

Cleaning and Defrosting

Defrosting is normally carried out when ice is $\frac{1}{4}$ inch thick. Manufacturers' instructions should be followed for occasional defrosting, but build-ups of ice may be removed with a plastic scraper. Sharp tools or wire brushes should not be used. For complete defrosting, food should be removed to a refrigerator or wrapped in layers of newspapers and blankets in a cold place. After defrosting, the freezer should be wiped completely dry and run at the coldest setting for 30 minutes before replacing food. The machine should then continue to run at the coldest setting for a further $2\frac{1}{2}$ hours before the switch is returned to normal setting.

The inside of the freezer is best cleaned with a solution of 1 quart water and 1 tablespoon bicarbonate of soda; the water should be lukewarm. Soap, detergent or caustic cleaners must not be used. The outside of the cabinet may be cleaned with warm soapy water and polished with enamel surface polish.

Power Failure

When power fails, the freezer is best checked first for local causes. The switch may have been turned off by mistake, or the fuse in the plug may have 'blown'.

The cabinet should be left shut when power has failed, so that the cold temperature is retained. Properly packed food will last about 12 hours safely, although this depends on the load of food and on insulation. A fully packed freezer will maintain a low temperature for a long period.

PACKING AND LABELLING

Freezing is not only an easy way of preserving both raw and cooked food, but it is also completely safe if the rules of hygiene are observed and food is correctly packed.

Good food will keep its quality and nutritive value in the freezer, but freezing cannot improve poor quality food.

Basic Freezing Procedure

1 All food for freezing must be processed quickly, according to the instructions.
2 Food must be thoroughly chilled before being put in the freezer to avoid raising the temperature of food already stored.
3 Food must be carefully packed to exclude air, and should be labelled for identification. A simple record of the food in the freezer will aid meal planning and encourage you to maintain a steady turnover.
4 Food should be frozen quickly, preferably against the cold surfaces of the cabinet, and at the recommended low temperature.
5 Frozen cooked food must never be thawed and then refrozen. Raw materials should not be thawed and refrozen, but may be made into cooked dishes and frozen.

Portions

Food should be prepared and packed in usable portions. Most people find it wise to prepare some large or family-sized packs and also a number of individual packs for use for single meals. Large packs of fruit and vegetables can be re-fastened after portions have been removed. A single portion of food will vary according to whether it is for a small child, a woman or a manual worker. Two people usually eat slightly less than two single portions when together.

Packaging Materials

All packaging should be moisture and vapour proof, waterproof and greaseproof; durable and resistant to low temperatures; easily handled, economically stored and free from smell. Suitable materials are indicated for various groups of foods; individual packing methods are described where necessary.

Waxed tubs Waxed tubs are available with flush airtight lids and with screw-on tops. Waxed cartons are also made with fitted lids in square and rectangular shapes, and there are tall containers with tuck-in lids, and special ones with polythene liners which are suitable for food subject to leakage.

Rigid plastic containers Most branded plastic boxes are suitable for freezer storage.

Fruit pie packed in a four-portion freezer tray.

Those with flexible sides can be lightly pressed to aid removal of contents. Special Swedish freezer boxes are available which can be boiled for sterilization and which stack and save space.

Glass jars Screwtop preserving jars, bottles and honey jars may be used for freezing if tested for resistance to low temperature. Place an empty jar in a plastic bag in the freezer overnight; if it breaks, the bag will hold the pieces. Jars with 'shoulders' should not be used as this necessitates long thawing before the food can be turned out and used.

If using freezer-to-table ware, remember that it is a bad conductor of heat. This means that dishes are slow in heating but hold their heat for a long time. Allow extra time for water, stock or sauces to reach boiling point, but in all cookery remove from the heat a short while before you would do so in other pans. It is difficult to halt the cooking even after removal from heat; sauces tend, therefore, to solidify or curdle, eggs harden and seared meats burn.

Polythene Polythene bags are useful for almost all freezer food, and are available in a wide variety of sizes; they should be of the special heavy quality designed for low temperatures. Polythene sheeting is easy to handle for wrapping meat, poultry and pies, and its transparency makes quick identification easy.

Foil and freezer paper Foil dishes are useful for dishes which are cooked before freezing and are later reheated, as one container may be used for all the processes. Heavy-duty foil sheeting is useful for overwrapping these dishes, and for packing both raw and cooked foods; it should be used with the dull side towards the food. Freezer paper is strong wrapping which is highly resistant to fat and grease, does not puncture easily, and has an uncoated outer surface on which labelling details may be written.

Various foil pans suitable for freezer use.

All types of container and sheet wrapping must be firmly sealed. Bags can be closed with fasteners or heat-sealed with a special welding unit, or with a domestic iron used over thick paper. Special deep-freezing tape with gum which is resistant to low temperatures must be used for finishing sheet-wrapped packages and sealing containers with lids.

Headspace and Air Exclusion

Containers with lids should be packed so that headspace from $\frac{1}{2}$ inch to 1 inch is left above the surface of the food to allow for expansion of contents, according to individual foods.

All sheet wrappings or bags must have the air pressed out so that the wrapping adheres closely to the food. When forming a parcel, the air can be pressed out with the hands. Air is most easily removed from bags by the insertion of a drinking straw at the closing, and by sucking the air out just before sealing.

Packaging

To avoid loss of quality, food should be carefully processed, packed, and then thawed or cooked quickly when needed. An enzyme is a type of protein which accelerates the chemical reactions in food. These reactions are slowed down by a freezing process, which is why freezing must be done quickly. Thawing speeds up enzymic reaction. It therefore encourages rapid deterioration, so that food is best thawed in a cold atmosphere such as a refrigerator, and must be eaten or cooked immediately after thawing.

Bad packaging causes a number of problems which will not render the food dangerous to eat, but which may cause an unattractive appearance, toughness and dryness, lack of flavour, or unpleasant mingling of flavours from different foods. Some of these are:
Dehydration and freezer burn Long storage and poor wrapping may result in the removal of moisture and juices, particularly from meat. This sometimes causes greyish-brown areas on food known as 'freezer burn'.

Oxidation and rancidity Oxygen from the air which penetrates wrappings reacts with fat cells in food to form chemicals which give meat and fish a bad taste and smell. Fried foods and fat meat and fish can suffer from this problem in the freezer. Salt accelerates this rancidity.

Broken packages and cross-flavourings Rough handling, sharp edges, brittle wrappings or overfilled containers may cause cracks or breakages which will result in dehydration or oxidation. This can also result in cross-flavouring with strongly flavoured foods, which may also spread smells and flavours if packages are not very strong or overwrapped.

Flabbiness Limp and flabby fruit and vegetables are caused by slow freezing, and sometimes by the choice of varieties unsuitable for freezing, which must be subject to trial and error. Suitable varieties are recommended on pages 36–44.

Ice crystals If too large a headspace is left on liquid foods in containers, a layer of ice crystals may form which will affect storage and flavour. Liquids can be shaken or stirred back into emulsion when heated or thawed. If the problem occurs in meat, fish, vegetables or fruit, it is usually because the food has been slow-frozen so that moisture in the cells has expanded and frozen and broken surrounding tissues. This results in juices and flavour being lost.

Suitable Packing Materials

The most commonly used packaging materials for various types of food are indicated thus *.

FOOD	WAXED OR RIGID PLASTIC CONTAINERS	FOIL CONTAINERS	FOIL SHEETING	POLYTHENE BAGS OR SHEETING
Fresh Meat			*	*
Fresh Poultry and Game			*	*
Fresh Fish			*	*
Cooked Meat and Fish Dishes	*	*	*	*
Fresh Vegetables	*			*
Fresh Vegetables (brine pack)	*			
Fresh Fruit (unsweetened or dry sugar pack)	*			*
Fresh Fruit (syrup pack)	*			
Butter, Margarine and Fats		*	*	*
Cheese			*	*
Milk and Cream	*			
Eggs	*	*		
Soups and Sauces	*	*	*	*
Bread, Cakes and Biscuits			*	*
Pastry and Pies		*	*	*
Desserts	*	*	*	*
Ice Cream	*		*	

PACKAGING HINTS

Preliminary Wrapping
It is important to attend to any preliminary wrapping of food so that items can be easily separated for thawing. Sliced meat should be layered with sheets of Cellophane or grease-proof paper to separate the slices; bones or protuberances on meat or poultry should be covered with a padding of paper or foil (see page 17); cakes without icing should be layered with separating paper.

Overwrapping
When packages are subject to heavy handling and possible puncture, or when there is danger of cross-flavouring, they should be overwrapped with ordinary brown paper, an extra layer of foil or polythene, or with stockinette (mutton cloth). An inside wrapping of stockinette on meat and poultry helps prevent freezer burn during long storage.

Sheet Wrapping
The food to be wrapped should be in the centre of the sheet of packaging material. Draw two sides of the sheet together above the food and fold them neatly downwards to bring the wrappings as close to the food as possible. Seal this fold, then fold ends like a parcel to make them close and tight, excluding air. Seal all folds and overwrap if necessary. This is sometimes called the 'druggist's wrap' or 'chemist's wrap'.

Bag Wrapping
Bags must be completely open before filling, and food must go down into corners, leaving no air pockets. A funnel is useful to avoid mess at the top of the bag. Bags can be sealed by heat or twist closing. For easier handling and storage, bags may be placed in other rigid containers for filling and freezing, then removed in a more compact form.

Heat Sealing
Polythene bags may be sealed by applying heat. This can be done with a special sealing iron or machine, but can also be handled with a domestic iron. When using a domestic iron, a thin strip of brown paper should be placed between the iron and the top of the polythene bag. It is important that all air should be excluded before sealing. Heat sealing gives a neat package which can be stored easily.

Twist Tying
All air should be extracted from the bag, and then a plastic-covered fastener twisted round the end of the bag. The top of the bag should then be turned down over this twist, and the fastener twisted again round the bunched neck of the bag. This gives a neat parcel, and ensures an airtight seal. It is sometimes known as a 'goose-neck closing'. Rubber bands are not recommended for this type of closing, as they perish at freezer temperatures.

Tape Sealing
Special freezer tape must be used. It should be applied to all containers with lids which do

Foil-wrapping of a stuffed fish for storage.

not have a special airtight seal, and to sheet-wrapped items. Tape should join the lid and container on cartons and plastic boxes, with an additional piece of tape over the lid to reach down the sides. On sheet-wrapped items, all folds must be taped so that all air is excluded.

Brick Freezing

When a large quantity of liquid such as stock or soup has to be frozen, freezer space can be wasted by using irregularly shaped containers. It is most practical to freeze this type of liquid in 'brick' form. The liquid can be poured into loaf tins of a convenient size, frozen, removed from the containers, and wrapped in freezer foil or polythene for easy storage.

Ice Cube Freezing

The same method can be used for freezing small quantities of liquid such as concentrated soups, sauces, fruit and vegetable purées, leftover tea and coffee, herbs, syrups and juices. The liquid should be poured into the ice cube trays and frozen without covering. Each cube should then be wrapped in foil and packed in quantities in a polythene bag for easy storage. The cubes can also be sprayed with soda water and packed in bulk, and will not stick together. Each cube will generally be enough for a single serving of the food.

LABELLING AND RECORDING

All items in the freezer should be labelled carefully, as many frozen items look alike after storage, particularly meat. Label with the name of the food, size of package in portions or by weight, and date of freezing. If possible include the date by which food should be eaten.

A two-section freezer tidily packed to save wasting space with food for a big party.

(See 'High quality storage life', page 24.) Add details of additional seasonings or other ingredients which must be added for serving, and of any planned accompaniments.

Labels must be written in felt pen, wax crayon or Chinagraph pencil, as other types of pen or pencil fade in the freezer. Labels can be written on tie-labels (which save additional closing wires), on labels treated with special adhesive which will stand sub-zero temperatures, or on paper tucked into transparent packages. It is easier to put stick-on labels on a package before filling it with food.

Recording
It is difficult to remember to keep records of food in the freezer, but it is essential to maintain some sort of record so that food is used in rotation while it is still of high quality. A plastic shopping list which can be wiped clean is easy to use. A book or card index is more difficult to maintain regularly. Record the food frozen, the number and size of packages, the date of freezing, the date by which food should be eaten, and the number of packets removed.

KEEPING THE FREEZER TIDY

It is much easier to use a freezer and maintain a regular turnover of food if the contents are kept tidy. An upright freezer is easier to organise because different shelves or drawers can be used for the various types of food. Avoid using cardboard boxes for storage as these take up a lot of space and become messy.

Baskets and Dividers
Plastic-covered wire mesh freezer baskets are available for hanging across the top of chest freezers and for use for stacking. Dividers are also available. This means that a main division can be made between meat and vegetables, for instance, or between raw materials and cooked foods.
NOTE: It must be remembered that baskets can be heavy to lift from the bottom of freezers when full of food.

Bags
Brightly-coloured mesh shopping bags are useful for keeping the freezer tidy. They can be filled with bag-wrapped food and with awkward-shaped parcels and are easy to lift. Large coloured polythene bags can also be used, but the contents are less easy to distinguish. Different colours of mesh or polythene bags can be used to identify types of food, such as fruit and vegetables.

Colour Coding
Identification of food can be greatly aided by using distinguishing colours. Bags, batching bags, labels and rigid boxes are available in six colours, so that one can identify different groups of food e.g. meat, vegetables, fruit; or a distinction can be made between different types of one food e.g. carrots, peas, beans.

HIGH QUALITY STORAGE LIFE

It is important that food stored in the freezer should not remain static; a good turnover should be maintained. Many foods can be stored for months in the freezer, but if they are kept too long colour, flavour and texture suffer. 'High Quality Storage Life' is the longest time food should be stored so that it is still perfect in every way when used. Cooked dishes in particular should be used within this storage time. Commercially-frozen packs should not be stored for longer than 3 months, and ice cream is best stored for no longer than 1 month.

It is a waste of valuable freezer space to store food beyond the end of the recommended storage life.

Remember that the wrong packaging material, bad packing and air spaces in the packs will affect the keeping qualities of frozen food. Salt, spices, herbs, onion and garlic flavours and fats also shorten the keeping time of foods as well as affecting flavours.

Item	High Quality Storage Life Number of Months	Item	High Quality Storage Life Number of Months
MEAT		FISH	
Beef	12	Oily Fish (Herring, Mackerel, Salmon, Trout)	2
Ham and Bacon (whole)	3	Shellfish	1
Ham and Bacon (sliced)	1	White Fish (Cod, Haddock, Plaice, Sole)	6
Lamb	9		
Minced Beef	2		
Offal	2	VEGETABLES	
Pork	6	Asparagus	9
Sausages and Sausage Meat	1	Beans	12
Veal	9	Brussels Sprouts	10
		Carrots	10
POULTRY		Fresh Herbs	10
Chicken	12	Part-Fried Chips	4
Duck	6	Peas	12
Giblets	3	Spinach	12
Goose	6	Tomatoes	6
Poultry Stuffing	1		
Turkey	6		
GAME			
Feathered Game	10		
Hare	6		
Rabbit	6		
Venison	12		

Item	High Quality Storage Life Number of Months	Item	High Quality Storage Life Number of Months
FRUIT		Fried Bread Shapes	1
Apricots	6	Fruit Pies	6
Cherries	7	Meat Pies	3
Currants	10	Pancakes (unfilled)	2
Fruit Juices	9	Pastry Cases	3
Fruit Purées	5	Pizza	1
Gooseberries	10	Plain Cakes	6
Melon	9	Sandwiches	2
Peaches	6	Savoury Flans	2
Plums	6	Unbaked Biscuits	4
Raspberries	12	Unbaked Bread, Rolls and Buns	2
Rhubarb	12	Unbaked Cakes	2
Strawberries	12	Unbaked Pastry	3
DAIRY PRODUCE		**COOKED DISHES**	
Double Cream	6	Casseroles and Stews	2
Eggs	12	Curry	2
Fresh Butter	6	Filled Pancakes	1
Hard Cheese	3	Fish Dishes	2
Ice Cream	1	Meat in Sauce	2
Salted Butter	3	Meat Loaf	1
Soft Cheese	6	Pâté	1
		Roast Meat	1
BAKERY GOODS		Sauces	2
Baked Bread, Rolls and Buns	2	Soufflés and Mousses	2
Breadcrumbs	3	Soup	2
Danish Pastry	1	Sponge Puddings	3
Decorated Cakes	3	Stock	2

FOODS TO AVOID FREEZING

Nearly all foods freeze well, but there are a few items to avoid completely, or to freeze only with great care. A few other foods cannot be frozen to eat raw, but can be used for cooking.

Here is a list of foods which are unsuitable for freezing:

Hard-boiled eggs (including Scotch eggs, eggs in pies and in sandwiches).

Soured cream and single cream (less than 40% butterfat) which separate.

Custards (including tarts). The custard mixture of eggs and milk can be frozen uncooked, but there is little point in this.

Soft meringue toppings.

Mayonnaise and salad dressings.

Milk puddings.

Royal icing and frostings without fat.

Salad vegetables with a high water content, e.g. lettuce, watercress, radishes.

Old boiled potatoes (potatoes can be frozen mashed, roast, baked or as chips).
Stuffed poultry.
Food with a high proportion of gelatine.
Whole eggs in shells which will crack (eggs can be frozen in packages).

Here is a list of foods to freeze with care:
Onions, garlic, spices and herbs. They sometimes get a musty flavour in cooked dishes in the freezer, and quantities should be reduced in such dishes as casseroles, and adjusted during reheating. Careful packing will help to prevent these strong flavours spreading to other food, and a short storage life is recommended.
Rice, spaghetti and potatoes should only be frozen without liquid. They become mushy in liquid and should not be frozen in soups or stews.
Sauces and gravy are best thickened by reduction, or with tomato or vegetable purée. If flour is used, it must be reheated with great care, preferably in a double saucepan, to avoid separation. Cornflour can be used but gives a glutinous quality. Egg and cream thickening should be added after freezing.
Bananas, apples, pears, whole melons and avocadoes cannot be successfully frozen whole to eat raw. They can be prepared in various ways for freezer storage (although pears are never very satisfactory). Bananas are not worth while as they are in season at a reasonable price throughout the year.
Cabbage cannot be frozen successfully to eat raw, and is not worth freezing as it occupies valuable freezer space. Red cabbage may be useful to keep frozen, as it has a short season and is never very plentiful.
Celery and chicory cannot be frozen to eat raw. They are useful to freeze in liquid to serve as vegetables. Celery can be used in stews or soup.
Tomatoes cannot be frozen to eat raw, but are invaluable in the freezer to use for soups, stews and sauces, or to freeze as purée or juice.
Milk must be homogenised and packed in waxed cartons. It is hardly worth bothering about as various types of milk can be stored without refrigeration.

BULK BUYING AND COOKING

BULK BUYING

Most people assume that buying in bulk will lead to a considerable saving in the family budget. Savings depend however on the number of people in the family, shopping and eating habits and the accessibility of shops. Freezer owners in fact find that they save on such hidden factors as public transport fares, or petrol and parking charges for cars, and they save a great deal of shopping time (which represents money). They also find that, although their overall shopping bills may remain the same, they tend to live better, since the price of better cuts of meat or out-of-season vegetables is balanced by freezing cheaper meat or home produce.

Factors Affecting Bulk Buying

It is a mistake to buy in bulk with price as the only consideration. This can result in poor quality food. For instance a cheap bag of prawns will probably have come from warmer waters and be tasteless compared with cold-water prawns from Greenland or Norway which are initially more expensive. In fact, the customer usually gets exactly what he pays for, and quality rarely combines with cheapness. When choosing a source of supply for buying food in bulk, therefore, it is worth considering the quality of the food, the service offered and the amount of food to be bought at one time.

It is also important to know the storage capacity of the freezer, and to judge how much space will be taken up by bulk purchases. About 20 lb. of frozen food will fit into 1 cu. ft. but a lot depends on the packaging and the shape of the food packages stored.

Some consideration must also be given to high quality storage life. There is little point in buying a gross of fish fingers for instance, if the family cannot eat these up within three months, as quality, flavour and texture deteriorate when the recommended storage life is exceeded.

How to Buy in Bulk

(a) **Check on savings of time or money.** Before making out bulk orders, check how the family money is spent and where the greatest savings can be made. Some bulk purchases, such as meat, save money. Other purchases, such as bread, save time. Some families hate spending time on shopping or cooking; so these factors should be considered when choosing the types of food to buy in bulk.

(b) **Check on quality.** Test small quantities of food before placing a large order. It is expensive, in the long run, if a bulk order of four dozen meat pies turns out to be unpopular with the family after one has been eaten. The remaining pies will take up valuable freezer space, and may put the whole family off this type of frozen food for keeps; little is lost by trying an individual item first.

Cheapness can also mean poor quality, so study order lists carefully. There may be half-a-dozen varieties of garden peas, for instance, and what looks like good value on paper can turn out to be very poor value indeed if the quality is low; much of the food may be wasted.

(c) Check on packaging. See that bulk food is properly packed for long-term storage. Food originally prepared for commercial and rapid use may come simply packed in cardboard boxes, or be slung into a polythene bag. A 7-lb. slab of pastry or 10 lb. minced meat clinging together in an enormous lump will be almost useless under home conditions. Be prepared to re-pack large purchases in usable quantities, as soon as the food is purchased. Check also whether it will be more convenient and cheaper in the long run to buy a bulk quantity of individual or family-size portions rather than enormous packs which are difficult to handle and store.

Where to Buy in Bulk

(a) Delivery Services. Some frozen food manufacturers and some freezer centres deliver in bulk to the door. This is a convenient way of ordering food since it can be transferred straight from the refrigerated van to storage, and it is particularly useful in country areas. A minimum order is normally stipulated, and it is worth preparing a bulk order with friends to make the delivery a worthwhile business. Sample small quantities of items which have not been bought before, and check delivery lists carefully to see that the order has been properly filled.

(b) Frozen Food Centres. These are found in many towns, and are useful for buying a wide variety of foods in both family and commercial pack sizes. They are useful places for trying new items before placing bulk orders, and the customer has the advantage of seeing and comparing the types of food. Try to choose a centre which is near a good parking space, and from which food can be taken home quickly. It is better to stick to reputable shops where the turnover is quick and the storage conditions are good. Some centres buy mainly on price and quality may be poor. Try to find the best shopping day for freezer centres when they take their main deliveries. It is not always a good idea to shop at a freezer centre on a Friday or Saturday, when most other people are shopping; stocks of popular items may be low, so that a planned list cannot be completely filled and valuable shopping time is wasted. Check also on highly seasonal items, particularly fruit. Popular fruits such as redcurrants and raspberries tend to be in short supply after a while, so if the family likes them, stock up in the summer when first supplies come in, since these fruits have a long storage life.

(c) Specialist Producers. Meat in particular is sold by specialist producers, either frozen or prepared for freezing. Such firms operate delivery services or express postal services, or food can be collected. The quality is usually high.

(d) Local Shops, Markets and Farms. Local shops and markets can usually supply fruit by the case and vegetables by the sack at reduced rates, as can local growers. A check should be kept on quality, as food may remain in shops for some days before sale. It is

Easy dishes for a fireworks party using commercially frozen products. The Apply Turnovers are just heated according to the manufacturers' instructions, while the others can be prepared quickly and simply (see recipes pp. 46, 79, 81, 109).

not a good idea to buy in this way if time is short, as there is a lot of labour involved in preparing a sack of vegetables for the freezer. Farmers often supply vegetables, fruit, meat or poultry, and fruit or vegetables are often very cheap if picked by the customer. Fish and shellfish are worth buying direct from the boat or from a seaside shop which has daily supplies. Home-baked bread, cakes and pies can often be obtained from local shops, W.I. stalls, etc. and some housewives undertake bulk cooking for the freezer.

What to Buy in Bulk
All types of food can be bought in bulk, but there is skill in choosing foods which the family will like and eat in quantity, and in balancing the quantities and types of food to be stored. Some savings may be in time, while other savings will be directly financial.

Bread and Cakes

Considerable time is saved by buying baked goods in bulk. This is an opportunity to buy crusty loaves; bread made from special flours; rolls and baps; sliced loaves for sandwiches and toast; buns; crumpets; malt and fruit loaves and cakes.

Convenience Foods

Food which has been prepared to save cooking and serving time is useful for quick meals, and particularly for in-between meals such as high tea for children which may not be required for the whole family. There are considerable savings in bulk packs of beefburgers, fish fingers, fishcakes, sausages, and thin cuts of meat and fish. Check the different kinds for variations in flavour and texture to see which are most popular with the family.

Prepared Dishes

Prepared pies, casseroles, puddings and gourmet dishes are useful for families which have little time for cooking. They should be bought in sizes most convenient for family use or for entertaining. Party dishes which need elaborate ingredients or lengthy cooking time are also useful. It is a good idea to buy small sizes first to see if they are acceptable.

Fruit and Vegetables

Farm or market produce can be home-frozen but takes time for preparation. It may be more useful to buy commercially-frozen fruit and vegetables in large packs. Particularly useful are such items as chips, mushrooms, green and red peppers, onions and mixed casserole vegetables. These are all in constant use in the kitchen, but are not always on hand in an accessible shop; nor are they particularly easy to prepare for freezing at home. Small quantities for recipe use can be shaken out of loose-packed commercial bags.

Ice Cream

Ice cream in bulk containers is useful for a family of children. The quality soon deteriorates if a container is frequently opened and 'scooped', and the product has a relatively short high quality storage life. So it may be more practical to buy bulk supplies of smaller packs, or of individual ices such as lollies and chocolate bars which are easy to serve and have a longer storage life.

Poultry

Whole birds and poultry pieces are very useful for adding variety to family menus, and prices are usually reasonable. They are very useful for converting into cooked dishes for the freezer for both family use and entertaining. Some farms and shops prepare free-range birds in quantity for home-freezing; others supply commercially-frozen poultry in bulk. It is best to pack giblets and livers separately in bulk for the freezer, as they do not store well inside birds, and are useful on their own for many recipes.

Meat

Meat is usually the most expensive item in the family budget, and is one of the most useful raw materials to buy in bulk. Bulk meat needs careful buying, and it is worth studying the problems before making an expensive purchase.

Chicken with Supreme Sauce, one of many excellent dishes that can be prepared using frozen chicken joints.

It is usually most practical to buy enough meat for the family's needs for three months, which is a reasonable turnover time and about the cheapest length of time to store the meat, allowing for the running costs of a freezer. It is a great mistake to purchase a quarter of beef, a pig and a lamb all at the same time, as novice freezer-owners tend to do. This overloads the freezer at the expense of other items, and pork in particular may deteriorate if kept beyond the recommended high quality storage life period. It is better to combine with one or two other families to get the advantage of bulk purchase with a variety of types of meat and different cuts.

Whole carcasses are ideal for those who will cook and eat cheaper cuts. Otherwise these will be wasted, and the roasting and grilling cuts will prove more expensive in the end. If a family only likes the better cuts, it is better to make a bulk purchase of these, or to buy a good variety pack of different meats. There will not be much financial saving, but there will be shopping convenience and no wastage. In bulk carcass buying, there may be considerable wastage in bones and suet; prices must be checked carefully to be sure the actual price of the meat used is not in excess of that quoted by the supplier.

Many experts do not recommend the home-freezing of meat at all. This is because meat must be frozen very quickly to retain its high quality, and commercial blast-freezing techniques give better results. If you do freeze meat at home, it is important to set the freezer correctly and only to freeze the recommended quantities at one time, and to label meat very carefully with the name of the cut and its possible uses. It is often better to choose the meat and have it frozen by the supplier. This does not apply, of course, to home-killed meat, or home-caught game and fish such as pheasants and salmon.

When buying meat, choose good quality, and see that it has been properly hung. See also that a list is made of all the cuts in the order and their possible uses (see tables for cuts of meat on pages 67–69), and also that they are packed in usable quantities. Get the meat properly prepared in the form in which it is wanted, either joints, steaks, casserole meat or mince. These specific points on our four principal meats are worth noting:

(a) **Beef** is a really bulky purchase. A forequarter will account for about 100 lb. and a hindquarter is even larger. The forequarter is more manageable, but consists mainly of slow-cooking cuts. Boned joints take up far less space in the freezer. The bones will account for about one-quarter of a bulk purchase, but can be made into concentrated stock for freezing (the butcher should be asked to saw them in reasonable pieces for the saucepan). Suet can be used for a wide variety of puddings, and can also be rendered down for fat. Check whether bones and suet are included in the overall price and if they will be delivered with the meat. Have the slow-cooking meat cut into slices and/or cubes for easy use, and ask for plenty of lean mince in 1 lb. packs which are very useful. Try to convert some of the cuts straight into pies or casseroles when they are delivered; this will save freezer space and provide some useful meals for quick use.

(b) **Veal** is not very often available in bulk, and is not very successful in the freezer, since it tends to lose flavour in storage conditions. If veal is bought, see that it is carefully divided into prepared boned roasting joints, escalopes and chops, and pie veal, etc. Remember that some veal bones, e.g. breast tendons, are a delicacy.

(c) **Lamb** is worth buying. A small lean one will weigh 25–30 lb. with little waste. Decide if you want chops in roasting joints or divided. If the cheaper chops and breast of lamb are not liked, it may be better value simply to buy roasting joints and bags of chops.

(d) **Pork** has a shorter storage life than other meats and should not be purchased in over-large quantities. Half a pig will weigh about 50 lb. and consists mostly of roasting and frying joints. The head and trotters may be included, but freezer space should not be wasted on them. They are better used at once in brawn or a dish which requires meat jelly.

Bulk Cooking

It can be all too easy to become a slave to the freezer, endlessly shopping and cooking to keep the white box topped up. It is important to take advantage of the fact that this is the only way of safely preserving cooked dishes. Cooking should be organised ahead so that two or three ready meals are always 'in hand' in the freezer. The great thing is to avoid inflicting the same kind of food on the family for weeks ahead, so new bulk purchases should be slightly different from the one recently made, and the cooked dishes used to vary those already in hand.

One of the greatest advantages of bulk cooking is that quantities of raw materials, such as bulk-bought meat, can be converted into cooked dishes as soon as they have been bought, saving considerable space. Stewing steak, for instance, can be made into casseroles and pies; mince can be converted into individual pies and shepherd's pies; chicken pieces can be used with a whole variety of sauces; offal can be made into casseroles and pâté.

For most people, it is best to double or treble quantities of such dishes as casseroles, using one immediately and saving the other portions for future use with added seasonings. Batch-baking is also sensible, to take full advantage of oven heat. It takes little more effort to make two cakes instead of one, or five dozen scones instead of one dozen. The same goes for pâtés, ice creams etc.

The Right Equipment

It pays to have the right-sized equipment and one or two labour-saving machines to use in conjunction with the freezer. Normal household equipment may not be suitable for bulk cooking.

(a) **Large saucepans** are useful not only for making stock, but for blanching vegetables, preparing fruit and meat. A large flat pan is useful for cooking ingredients in fat at the first stages of many recipes.

(b) **Large casseroles** are another essential. At least one 6–8 pint size is needed for bulk cooking, or a large double roaster.

(c) **A pressure cooker** speeds up the cooking of meat and poultry in particular. It can also double as an ordinary large pan.

(d) **An electric mixer with attachments** is invaluable in cooking for the freezer. The mixer itself is useful for making all types of cakes, and for beating ice cream and whipping up puddings. The blender attachment, or an independent blender, is useful for soups, purées and sauces. A mincer attachment aids the making of mince and sausages from bulk-bought meat, and speeds up pâté-making. A slicing attachment is handy for preparing vegetables, and a dough-hook is useful for yeast doughs for bread, buns and pizza.

An adequate oven is necessary to take batch-baking, etc. If a new one is being purchased, see that there is plenty of oven space, and if possible buy a cooker with a fan-assisted oven. This ensures that heat is circulated and a steady baking temperature is maintained throughout the oven. Cooks who have an Aga or similar stove with two ovens are fortunate, as different types of dishes can be cooked at the same time.

What to Cook for Freezing   Before cooking foods for freezing, it is wise to assess which items are worth freezer space. Briefly, these are:

(a) Dishes which need long cooking or long and tedious preparation.

(b) Dishes made from seasonal foods.

(c) Dishes which can be made in large quantities with little more work (i.e. three cakes instead of one; double or treble casseroles).

(d) Dishes for special occasions, such as parties or holidays.

(e) Convenience foods for invalids, small children, unexpected illness.

FREEZING VEGETABLES AND HERBS

All vegetables to be frozen should be young and tender, and they are best picked and frozen in small amounts. Shop-bought vegetables are generally too old to be worth freezing, but a few seasonal delicacies such as aubergines and peppers are worth the trouble of preparing them.

Vegetables to be frozen must be blanched to arrest the working of enzymes (types of protein in foods which speed up chemical reactions). Blanching at high heat stops the enzymes from affecting quality, flavour, colour and nutritive value during storage. Unblanched vegetables can be stored for up to three months in the freezer, but the effect of freezing will be the same as that of an early frost, and they will lose their colour and texture. Unblanched vegetables also require the full cooking time, unlike blanched vegetables which are already partly cooked.

Preparation for Freezing

All vegetables must first be washed thoroughly in cold water, then cut or sorted into similar sizes. If more are picked than can be dealt with, they should be put into polythene bags in a refrigerator.

Blanching

There are two forms of blanching, (a) by water; (b) by steam. Steam blanching is not recommended for leafy green vegetables which tend to mat together, and it takes longer than water blanching, though it conserves more minerals and vitamins. Blanching should be timed carefully, though inaccuracy will not be disastrous. Too little blanching may result in colour change and in a loss of nutritive value; too much blanching will mean a loss of crispness and fresh flavour.

(a) **Water blanching.** Blanch only 1 lb. vegetables at a time to ensure thoroughness and to prevent a quick change in the temperature of the water. Use a saucepan holding at least 8 pints of water. Bring the water to the boil while the vegetables are being prepared. Put vegetables into a wire basket, chip pan, salad shaker or a muslin bag and completely immerse in the saucepan of fast-boiling water; cover tightly and keep the heat high under the saucepan until blanching is completed. Check carefully the time needed for each vegetable (see below, pages 36–44) and time blanching from when water returns to boiling point. As soon as the full blanching time has elapsed, remove vegetables and drain at once. Bring water to boiling point again before dealing with another batch of vegetables.

(b) **Steam blanching.** Put enough water into the saucepan below a steamer to prevent any risk of it boiling dry. Prepare the vegetables, and when the water is boiling fast put

Mixed Vegetables diced in even slices for freezing.

the wire basket or muslin bag into steamer. Cover tightly, and count steaming time from when the steam escapes from the lid. Steam blanching takes half as long again as water blanching (e.g. 2 minutes water blanching equals 3 minutes steam blanching).

Cooling

Cooling must be done immediately after blanching, and it must be very thorough indeed; before being packed for the freezer, the vegetables should be cool right through to the centre. The time taken is generally equal to the blanching time if a large quantity of cold water is used. It is best to ice-chill this water, and it is a good idea to prepare large quantities of ice the day before a vegetable freezing session is planned. Vegetables which are not cooled quickly become mushy as they will go on cooking in their own heat. After cooling in the water, the vegetables should be thoroughly drained, and preferably finished off on absorbent paper.

Packing

Pack the cooled food in usable quantities to suit family or entertaining needs (see above, page 16). Vegetables can be packed in bags or boxes; the chosen method will depend on the storage space available, as bagged vegetables are more difficult to keep though obviously cheaper to prepare.

Vegetables are normally packed dry, though wet-packing in brine is believed to prevent some vegetables toughening in storage, and non-leafy varieties can be packed in this way. The vegetables are packed into rigid containers to within 1 in. of the top, and are then just covered with brine, made in the proportion of 2 tablespoons salt per quart of water,

35

leaving $\frac{1}{2}$ in. headspace. It may be found in hard water areas that home-frozen vegetables are consistently tough, and it is then worth experimenting with this brine method.

Cooking

The best results are obtained from cooking vegetables immediately on removal from the freezer. When cooking unthawed vegetables, break the blocks into 4 or 5 pieces when removing from the carton, to allow heat to penetrate evenly and rapidly.

One or two vegetables such as broccoli and spinach are better cooked partially thawed, and corn on the cob needs complete thawing. Mushrooms should be cooked frozen; they become pulpy when thawed. If vegetables are thawed, they should be cooked at once.

Partial cooking during blanching, and the tenderising process produced by temperature changes during storage, reduce the final cooking time of frozen vegetables. In general, they should cook in one-third to one-half the time allowed for fresh vegetables. Very little water, if any, should be used for cooking frozen vegetables; about $\frac{1}{4}$ pint to 1 lb. vegetables, depending on variety, is plenty. The water should be boiling, the vegetables covered at once with a lid, and as soon as boiling point is reached again, the vegetables should be simmered gently for the required time. Since flavour is always lost into the cooking water, some cooks prefer to steam vegetables, cook them in a double boiler, or to bake or fry them. For baking, the vegetables should be separated and drained, then put into a greased casserole with a knob of butter and seasoning, covered tightly and baked at 350° F (Gas Mark 4) for about 30 minutes. For frying, the vegetables remain frozen, and are put into a heavy frying pan containing 1 oz melted butter. The pan must be tightly covered and the vegetables cooked gently until they separate, then cooked over moderate heat until cooked through and tender, being turned as required to prevent burning.

Here are notes on preparing, packing, storing and cooking various kinds of vegetables. The blanching times given are for water blanching:

Artichokes (Globe)

Preparation   (a) Remove outer leaves. Wash, trim stalks and remove 'chokes'. Blanch in 8 pints water with 1 tablespoon lemon juice for 7 minutes. Cool and drain upside down. Pack in boxes. (b) Remove all green leaves and 'chokes'. Blanch artichoke hearts for 5 minutes.

Serving   (a) Cook in boiling water for 5 minutes. (b) Use as fresh artichokes for special dishes.
High Quality Storage Life   (a) 12 months, (b) 12 months

Artichokes (Jerusalem)

Preparation   Peel and cut in slices. Soften in a little butter, and simmer in a chicken stock. Rub through a sieve and pack in boxes.

Serving   Use as a basis for soup with milk or cream and seasoning.
High Quality Storage Life   3 months

Asparagus

Preparation   Wash and remove woody portions and scales. Grade for size and cut in 6 in. lengths. Blanch 2 minutes (small spears); 3 minutes (medium spears); 4 minutes (large spears). Cool and drain. Pack in boxes.

Serving   Cook 5 minutes in boiling water.
High Quality Storage Life   9 months

Aubergines

Preparation   Use mature, tender, medium-sized. (a) Peel and cut in 1 in. slices. Blanch 4 minutes, chill and drain. Pack in layers separated by paper in boxes. (b) Coat slices in thin batter, or egg and breadcrumbs. Deep-fry, drain and cool. Pack in layers in boxes.

Serving   (a) Cook 5 minutes in boiling water, (b) Heat in a slow oven or part thaw and deep-fry.
High Quality Storage Life   (a) 12 months, (b) 1 month

Beans (Broad)

Preparation   Use small young beans. Shell and blanch for $1\frac{1}{2}$ minutes. Pack in bags or boxes.

Serving   Cook 8 minutes in boiling water.
High Quality Storage Life   12 months

Beans (French)

Preparation   Remove tops and tails. Leave small beans whole; cut larger ones into 1 in. pieces. Blanch 3 minutes (whole beans); 2 minutes (cut beans). Cool and pack in bags.

Serving   Cook 7 minutes in boiling water (whole beans); 5 minutes (cut beans).
High Quality Storage Life   12 months

Beans (Runner)

Preparation   Do not shred, but cut in pieces and blanch 2 minutes. Cool and pack.

Serving   Cook 7 minutes in boiling water.
High Quality Storage Life   12 months

Beetroot

Preparation Use very young beetroot, under 3 in. across. They must be completely cooked in boiling water until tender. Rub off skins and pack in boxes, either whole or cut in slices or dice.

Serving Thaw 2 hours in container in refrigerator. Drain and add dressing.
High Quality Storage Life 6 months

Broccoli

Preparation Use green, compact heads with tender stalks 1 in. thick or less. Trim stalks and remove outer leaves. Wash well and soak in salt water for 30 minutes (2 teaspoons salt to 8 pints water). Wash in fresh water, and cut into sprigs. Blanch 3 minutes (thin stems); 4 minutes (5 minutes thick stems). Pack into boxes or bags, alternating heads.

Serving Cook 8 minutes in boiling water.
High Quality Storage Life 12 months

Brussels Sprouts

Preparation Grade small compact heads. Clean and wash well. Blanch 3 minutes (small); 4 minutes (medium). Cool and pack in bags or boxes.

Serving Cook 8 minutes in boiling water.
High Quality Storage Life 12 months

Cabbage (Green and Red)

Preparation Use crisp young cabbage. Wash and shred finely. Blanch 1½ minutes. Pack in bags.

Serving Cook 8 minutes in boiling water. Do not use raw.
High Quality Storage Life 6 months

Carrots

Preparation Use very young carrots. Wash and scrape. Blanch 3 minutes for small whole carrots, sliced or diced carrots. Pack in bags or boxes.

Serving Cook 8 minutes in boiling water.
High Quality Storage Life 12 months

Cauliflower

Preparation Use firm compact heads with close white flowers. Wash and break into sprigs. Blanch 3 minutes in 8 pints water with 1 tablespoon lemon juice. Cool and pack in lined boxes or bags.

Serving Cook 10 minutes in boiling water.
High Quality Storage Life 6 months

Celery

Preparation (a) Use crisp young stalks. Scrub well and remove strings. Cut in 1 in. lengths and blanch 2 minutes. Cool and drain and pack in bags. (b) Prepare as above, but pack in boxes with water used for blanching, leaving $\frac{1}{2}$ in. headspace.

Serving Use as a vegetable, or for stews or soups, using liquid if available. Do not use raw.
High Quality Storage Life 6 months

Chestnuts

Preparation Bring chestnuts in shells to the boil. Drain and peel off shells. Pack in boxes or bags.

Serving Cook in boiling water or milk, according to recipe.
High Quality Storage Life 6 months

Chicory

Preparation Wash well and remove outer leaves. Blanch 3 minutes and cool in cooking liquid. Pack in the blanching liquid in boxes, leaving $\frac{1}{2}$ in. headspace.

Serving Put into a covered dish in the oven in blanching liquid and heat at 350°F (Gas Mark 4) for 40 minutes. Drain and serve with butter.
High Quality Storage Life 6 months

Corn on the Cob

Preparation (a) Use fresh tender corn. Remove leaves and threads and grade cobs for size. Blanch 4 minutes (small cobs); 6 minutes (medium cobs); 8 minutes (large cobs). Cool and dry. Pack individually in foil or freezer paper. Freeze and pack in bags for storage. (b) Blanch cobs and scrape off kernels. Pack in boxes, leaving $\frac{1}{2}$ in. headspace.

Boiled corn on the cob to be served with melted butter.

Serving　(a) Thaw before cooking. Put cobs in cold water, bring to a fast boil and simmer 5 minutes. (b) Thaw in wrappings in refrigerator. Cook 10 minutes in boiling water.
High Quality Storage Life　12 months

Cucumber

Preparation　Cut in thin slices and pack in boxes. Cover with equal quantities white vinegar and water, seasoned with ½ teaspoon sugar and 1 teaspoon black pepper to 1 pint liquid.

Serving　Thaw in container in refrigerator. Drain and season with salt.
High Quality Storage Life　2 months

Fennel

Preparation　Use crisp young stalks. Scrub well. Blanch 3 minutes. Cool and pack in blanching water in boxes.

Serving　Simmer 30 minutes in blanching water or stock. Slip hard cores from roots when cooked.
High Quality Storage Life　6 months

40

Herbs (Mint, Parsley and Chives)

Preparation (a) Wash and pack sprigs in bags. (b) Chop finely and pack into ice-cube trays. Transfer frozen cubes to bags for storage.

Serving Thaw at room temperature for sandwich fillings. Add cubes to sauces, soups or stews. Do not use for garnish.
High Quality Storage Life 6 months

Kale

Preparation Use young, tender kale. Remove dry or tough leaves. Strip leaves from stems and blanch 1 minute. Cool and drain. Chop leaves for convenient packing. Pack into bags.

Serving Cook 8 minutes in boiling water.
High Quality Storage Life 6 months

Kohlrabi

Preparation Use young and tender, not too large, and mild-flavoured. Trim, wash and peel. Small ones may be frozen whole, but large ones should be diced. Blanch 3 minutes (whole); 2 minutes (diced). Cool and pack in bags or boxes.

Serving Cook 10 minutes in boiling water.
High Quality Storage Life 12 months

Leeks

Preparation Trim off roots and green stems. Wash very well and remove dirty outer layers. Cut either finely or coarsely into even lengths. Blanch finely-cut leeks for 1½ minutes; coarsely-cut leeks for 3 minutes. Cool thoroughly and drain, or pack in blanching liquid.

Serving Cook drained leeks until tender in salted water, and serve with butter or sauce, or make into a purée, or add to a soup or stew. Leeks packed in blanching liquid can be used to make soup.
High Quality Storage Life 12 months

Marrow

Preparation (a) Cut young marrows or courgettes in ½ in. slices without peeling. Blanch 3 minutes and pack in boxes, leaving ½ in. headspace. (b) Peel and seed large marrows. Cook until soft, mash and pack in boxes.

Serving (a) Fry in oil, and season well. (b) Reheat in double boiler with butter and seasoning.
High Quality Storage Life 6 months

Mushrooms

Preparation (a) Wipe but do not peel. Cut large mushrooms in slices. Stalks may be frozen separately. Blanch $1\frac{1}{2}$ minutes in 6 pints water with 1 tablespoon lemon juice. Pack cups down in boxes, leaving $1\frac{1}{2}$ in. headspace. (b) Grade and cook in butter for 5 minutes. Allow 6 tablespoons butter to 1 lb. mushrooms. Cool quickly, take off excess fat, and pack in boxes.

Serving (a) Thaw in container in refrigerator, and cook in butter. (b) Add while frozen to soups, stews or other dishes.
High Quality Storage Life (a) 3 months, (b) 2 months

Onions

Preparation (a) Peel, chop and pack in small boxes. Overwrap. (b) Cut in slices and wrap in foil or freezer paper, dividing layers with paper. Overwrap. (c) Chop or slice, blanch 2 minutes. Cool and drain. Pack in boxes. Overwrap. (d) Leave tiny onions whole. Blanch 4 minutes. Pack in boxes. Overwrap.

Serving Thaw raw onions in refrigerator. Add to salads while frosty. Add frozen onions to dishes according to recipe.
High Quality Storage Life 2 months

Parsnips

Preparation Use young parsnips. Trim and peel. Cut into narrow strips or dice. Blanch 2 minutes. Pack in bags or boxes.

Serving Cook 15 minutes in boiling water.
High Quality Storage Life 12 months

Peas, Green

Preparation Use young sweet peas. Shell. Blanch 1 minute, shaking basket to distribute heat. Cool and drain. Pack in boxes or bags.

Serving Cook 7 minutes in boiling water.
High Quality Storage Life 12 months

Peas (Edible Pods)

Preparation Use flat tender pods. Wash well. Remove ends and strings. Blanch $\frac{1}{2}$ minute in small quantities.

Serving Cook 7 minutes in boiling water.
High Quality Storage Life 12 months

Peppers (Green and Red)

Preparation   (a) Wash well. Cut off stems and caps, and remove seeds and membranes. Blanch 2 minutes (slices); 3 minutes (halves). Pack in boxes or bags. (b) Grill on high heat until skin is charred. Plunge into cold water and rub off skins. Remove caps and seeds. Pack tightly in boxes in salt solution (1 tablespoon salt to 1 pint water), leaving 1 in. headspace.

Serving   (a) Thaw 1½ hours at room temperature. (b) Thaw in liquid and drain. Dress with oil and seasoning.
High Quality Storage Life   12 months

Potatoes

Preparation   (a) Scrape and wash new potatoes. Blanch 4 minutes. Cool and pack in bags. (b) Slightly undercook new potatoes. Drain, toss in butter, cool and pack in bags. (c) Mash potatoes with butter and hot milk. Pack in boxes or bags. (d) Form potatoes into croquettes or Duchesse Potatoes. Cook, cool and pack in boxes. (e) Fry chips in clean fat for 4 minutes. Do not brown. Cool and pack in bags.

Serving   (a) Cook 15 minutes in boiling water. (b) Plunge bag in boiling water. Take off heat and leave 10 minutes. (c) Reheat in double boiler. (d) Thaw 2 hours. Heat at 350°F, 180°C (Gas Mark 4) for 20 minutes. (e) Fry in deep fat.
High Quality Storage Life   (a) 12 months, (b) 3 months, (c) 3 months, (d) 3 months, (e) 3 months

Pumpkin

Preparation   Peel and seed. Cook until soft. Mash and pack in boxes.

Serving   (a) Reheat in double boiler with butter and seasoning. (b) Thaw 2 hours at room temperature and use as a pie filling.
High Quality Storage Life   6 months

Spinach

Preparation   Use young tender spinach. Remove stems. Wash very well. Blanch 2 minutes, shaking basket so the leaves separate. Cool and press out moisture. Pack in boxes or bags.

Serving   Melt a little butter and cook frozen spinach 7 minutes.
High Quality Storage Life   12 months

Tomatoes

Preparation (a) Wipe tomatoes and remove stems. Grade and pack in small quantities in bags. (b) Skin and core tomatoes. Simmer in own juice for 5 minutes until soft. Sieve, cool and pack in boxes. (c) Core tomatoes and cut in quarters. Simmer with lid on for 10 minutes. Put through muslin. Cool juice and pack in boxes, leaving 1 in. headspace.

Serving (a) Thaw 2 hours at room temperature, skins slip off when thawed. Grill, or use in recipes. Do not use raw. (b) Thaw 2 hours at room temperature. Use for soups or stews. (c) Thaw in refrigerator. Serve frosty. Add seasoning.
High Quality Storage Life   12 months

Turnips

Preparation (a) Use small, young mild turnips. Peel and cut in dice. Blanch $2\frac{1}{2}$ minutes. Cool and pack in boxes. (b) Cook turnips until tender. Drain and mash. Pack in boxes, leaving $\frac{1}{2}$ in. headspace.

Serving (a) Cook 10 minutes in boiling water. (b) Reheat in double boiler with butter and seasoning.
High Quality Storage Life   (a) 12 months, (b) 3 months

Vegetables (Mixed)

Preparation Prepare and blanch vegetables separately. Mix and pack in boxes.

Serving Cook 7 minutes in boiling water.
High Quality Storage Life   12 months

Vegetable Purée

Preparation Cook and sieve vegetables. Pack in boxes. Small quantities can be frozen in ice-cube trays, and the cubes transferred to bags for easy storage.

Serving Add to soups. Purée may be reheated in a double boiler.
High Quality Storage Life   3 months

Vegetables in Sauce

Preparation Slightly undercook vegetables. Cool and fold into sauce. Pack into boxes.

Serving Reheat in double boiler.
High Quality Storage Life   2 months

The following recipes based on vegetables freeze well:

Leek Soup

4 leeks
1 oz butter
1 pint chicken stock

Clean leeks thoroughly and cut into thin rings. Melt butter, and soften leeks without colouring them. Add stock, season lightly and simmer for 30 minutes. Cool. Pack in waxed or rigid plastic container, leaving headspace.

To serve
Reheat gently, adjust seasoning, and stir in $\frac{1}{4}$ pint creamy milk. Garnish with chopped parsley or chives.
High Quality Storage Life　1 month

Onion Soup

$1\frac{1}{2}$ lb onions
2 oz butter
3 pints beef stock
Salt and pepper
2 tablespoons cornflour

Slice the onions finely and cook gently in butter until soft and golden. Add stock and seasoning, bring to the boil, and simmer for 20 minutes. Thicken with cornflour and simmer for 5 minutes. Pack after cooling and removing fat, into containers, leaving headspace.

To serve
Reheat in double boiler, stirring gently. Meanwhile, spread slices of French bread with butter and grated cheese, and toast until cheese has melted. Put slices into tureen or individual bowls and pour over soup.
High Quality Storage Life　2 months

Iced Tomato Soup

8 thinly-sliced tomatoes
4 thinly-sliced small
　white onions
4 peeled and finely-
　chopped cloves garlic
Strip of lemon rind
4 tablespoons water
6 tablespoons tomato
　paste
4 tablespoons flour
1 pint chicken stock
1 teaspoon Tabasco
　Sauce
1 teaspoon sugar
Salt and pepper
2 tablespoons sherry
　(optional)
1 teaspoon lemon juice
$\frac{1}{4}$ pint single cream

Combine thinly sliced tomatoes and onions, chopped garlic, lemon rind and water and simmer gently for 10–15 minutes. Add tomato paste and cook a further three minutes. Stir in flour made into a paste in some of the measured stock. Add remaining stock, Tabasco sauce, sugar, salt and pepper. Bring soup to the boil stirring constantly. Sieve the soup through a fine strainer. Add sherry and lemon juice. Pack into rigid container, leaving headspace, and freeze.

To serve
Thaw in refrigerator for 3 hours. Stir in cream and serve garnished with thin cucumber slices.
High Quality Storage Life　1 month

Minestrone Soup

8 oz lean beef
2 pints water
1 carrot
1 onion
1 small turnip
4 tomatoes
2 stalks celery (with
   leaves)
2 oz shelled peas
2 oz soaked haricot
   beans
Salt and pepper

Mince the meat, using a coarse screen. Chop the skinned tomatoes, celery tops, carrot, onion and turnip finely. Put into a pan with the meat, peas, celery stalks cut into $\frac{1}{2}$-in. pieces and the haricot beans. Add the water, bring to the boil and simmer for 1 hour. Season lightly with salt and pepper, cool and pack in containers, leaving headspace.

To serve
Reheat and add 2 oz pasta which has been cooked in a separate pan for 5 minutes. Simmer for 10 minutes and serve with plenty of Parmesan cheese.
High Quality Storage Life   2 months

Mixed Vegetable Soup

1 oz butter
1 oz flour
2 pints beef stock
1 lb frozen vegetables
Salt and pepper
Sprig of parsley

Melt butter in saucepan, stir in flour and cook gently for 1 minute. Add stock and bring to boil, stirring. Add mixed vegetables and simmer for 15 minutes. Serve hot, garnish with parsley.

46

Duchesse Potatoes

2 lb cooked potatoes
4 oz butter
2 eggs
Salt and pepper
Pinch of nutmeg

Put potatoes through a sieve, and beat well with butter and eggs to give a piping consistency, seasoning well. A little hot milk may be added if mixture is stiff. Pipe in pyramids on to baking sheets lined with oiled paper. Pack frozen shapes into bags of suitable quantities.

To serve
Put on to baking sheets, brush with egg and cook at 400°F, 200°C, Gas Mark 6, for 20 minutes.
High Quality Storage Life 1 month

Creamed Spinach

Spinach leaves
2 oz butter
1 oz flour
¼ pint milk
Top of milk or cream
Sea-salt

Wash leaves well. Cook gently in a large saucepan with water. Turn from time to time until tender. Drain. In same saucepan melt butter, add flour and milk to make a thick white sauce. Return spinach to saucepan and mix very thoroughly, cutting with a knife against the side of the pan. Finally add top of milk or cream. Freeze in cartons.

To serve
Reheat in a double boiler stirring gently.
High Quality Storage Life 2 months

Summer Ratatouille

2 medium onions
1 lb tomatoes
3 small aubergines
2 small green or red peppers
4 small courgettes
2 cloves garlic, peeled and crushed
3 tablespoons olive oil
Salt
¼ teaspoon Tabasco sauce
12 coriander seeds

Chop the onions and skin the tomatoes. Cut the aubergines into ½-in. dice, place in a colander and sprinkle with salt. Seed and cut the peppers into dice. Slice the courgettes into ¼-in. slices. Gently cook the chopped onion and crushed garlic in the oil. Rinse the aubergines and dry on kitchen paper. Add to the onion with courgettes, tomatoes and peppers. Season with salt and pepper sauce. Add the coriander seeds, cover closely and simmer very slowly for 40 minutes. Cool and freeze.

To serve
Thaw at room temperature for 3 hours. Garnish with chopped parsley.
High Quality Storage Life 2 months

Green Pepper Sauce

2 tablespoons dripping
1 large green pepper
1 large onion
½ teaspoon garlic salt
1 tablespoon cornflour
½ pint meat stock
16-oz can tomatoes

Melt the dripping and add the sliced pepper and onion and the garlic salt. Cook until tender. Blend the cornflour with the stock and add to the sauce. Boil for 1 minute. Stir in the tomatoes with their juice. Simmer for 5 minutes, cool and pack into a rigid container.

To serve
Reheat in a double saucepan, or in a bowl over hot water.
High Quality Storage Life   2 months

Tomato Sauce

1 lb tomatoes
1 oz butter
1 small onion
1 small carrot
1 oz ham
1 pint stock
Parsley, thyme, bay leaf
1 oz cornflour

Cut tomatoes in slices. Melt butter and fry sliced onion and carrot until golden. Add tomatoes, ham, stock and herbs and simmer for 30 minutes. Put through a sieve, thicken with cornflour, season again to taste, and cook for 5 minutes stirring well. Cool. Pack in containers, in brick form, or in ice cube trays, wrapping bricks or cubes when frozen in foil.

To serve
Thaw in double boiler, stirring gently.
High Quality Storage Life   12 months

Parsley Butter

2 oz butter
2 teaspoons lemon juice
2 teaspoons chopped
   parsley
Salt and pepper

Cream butter and work in other ingredients. Form butter into a roll, wrap in greaseproof paper and polythene and freeze.

To serve
Cut off in slices when required to serve with grilled meat or fish.
High Quality Storage Life   2 months

Tomato Juice

Use ripe tomatoes, core and quarter them, and simmer them with a lid on, but with no liquid, for 10 minutes. Put through muslin, cool and pack into cartons, leaving 1 in. headspace.

To serve
Thaw juice for 1 hour in container in the refrigerator, and season with salt, pepper and a squeeze of lemon juice.
High Quality Storage Life   1 year

FREEZING FRUIT

The best results are obtained from fully-flavoured fruits, particularly berries. The blander fruits such as pears are satisfactory, but have little flavour. In general, fruit for freezing should be of top quality; over-ripe fruit will be mushy (though it may be possible to store as purée); unripe fruit will be tasteless and poorly-coloured.

It is important to work quickly when preparing fruit; home-picked fruit should be frozen on the same day, while fruit from shop or market should only be bought in manageable quantities which can be handled in a short space of time.

Whichever method of packing is to be used, wash the fruit in plenty of water containing ice cubes as this will prevent the fruit becoming soggy and losing juice. Fruit should be drained immediately in an enamel, aluminium, stainless steel or earthenware container (avoid copper, iron and galvanised ware which produce off-flavours), and may be further drained on absorbent paper. It is important to be gentle in removing stems or stones from fruit to be frozen; this should be done with the tips of the fingers, without squeezing.

Fruit Freezing Methods

Unsweetened Dry Pack

This pack can be used for fruit for use in pies, puddings and jams, or for people on a sugar-free diet. It should not be used for fruit which discolours badly during preparation, as sugar helps to retard the action of the enzymes which cause darkening.

To pack fruit by this method, wash and drain and pack into cartons. Do not use excess water in cleaning the fruit. Seal and freeze and label carefully. For an unsweetened pack, it is even better to open-freeze fruit. Spread it out on metal or plastic trays for fast-freezing. When frozen, pour into polythene bags or boxes for storage. Small quantities can easily be shaken out for use.

Unsweetened Wet Pack

This method is little used, but is acceptable for very sweet fruit or for puddings to be made for people on a diet. The fruit should be packed in liquid-proof containers, either gently crushed in its own juice, or covered with water to which lemon juice has been added to prevent discolouration (juice of 1 lemon to $1\frac{1}{2}$ pints water). If the fruit is tart but no sugar is to be used, it may be frozen in water sweetened with a sugar substitute, or with a sugar-free carbonated beverage. Seal, freeze and label carefully.

Dry Sugar Pack

This is a good method for crushed or sliced fruit, or for soft juicy fruit from which the

A frozen flan case filled with redcurrants frozen separately in a dry sugar pack (see p. 55).

juice draws easily such as berries. The fruit should be washed and drained and may be packed by two methods: (a) mix fruit and sugar in a bowl with a silver spoon, adjusting sweetening to tartness of fruit (average 3 lb. fruit to 1 lb. sugar). Pack fruit into containers, leaving $\frac{1}{2}$ in. headspace, seal and freeze, and label carefully: (b) pack fruit in layers, using the same proportion of fruit and sugar; start with a layer of fruit, sprinkle with sugar, then more fruit and sugar, leaving $\frac{1}{2}$ in. headspace. Seal and freeze, labelling carefully.

Syrup Pack

This method is best for non-juicy fruits, and those which discolour easily. Syrup is normally made from white sugar and water. (For those who dislike white sugar for dietary reasons, honey may be used, but it flavours the fruit strongly. Brown sugar may likewise be used, but affects the colour of the fruit.)

The syrup is referred to as a percentage, according to the amount of sugar and water used. A medium syrup or 40% syrup is best for most purposes as a heavier syrup tends to make the fruit flabby. The sugar must be completely dissolved in boiling water, then cooled. It must be completely cold before adding it to the fruit, and it is best stored in a refrigerator for a day before using. The fruit should be packed into containers and covered with syrup, leaving $\frac{1}{2}$–1 in. headspace. To prevent discolouration, a piece of Cellophane should be pressed down over the fruit into the syrup before sealing, freezing and labelling.

Syrup

Sugar	Water	Type of Syrup
4 oz	1 pint	20% very light syrup
7 oz	1 pint	30% light syrup
11 oz	1 pint	40% medium syrup
16 oz	1 pint	50% heavy syrup
25 oz	1 pint	60% very heavy syrup

Headspace

Headspace must be allowed for all fruit in sugar or syrup, for juice or purée: $\frac{1}{2}$ in. should be allowed for all dry packs; $\frac{1}{2}$–1 in. per pint for wide-topped wet packs and $\frac{3}{4}$–1 in. per pint for narrow-topped wet packs. Double headspace is needed for quart containers.

Discolouration

Discolouration is the greatest problem in fruit packing for freezing. Apples, peaches and pears are particularly subject to this during preparation, storage and thawing. In general, fruit which has a lot of Vitamin C darkens less easily, so adding lemon juice or citric acid to the sugar pack will help to arrest darkening. Use the juice of 1 lemon to 1$\frac{1}{2}$ pints water, or 1 teaspoon citric acid to each 1 lb. of sugar in dry pack. Ascorbic acid can likewise be used; it can be bought in tablet or crystalline form from the chemist. 500 milligrammes or 1 tablet of ascorbic acid should be used for 1 pint of water (1 teaspoon of the acid equals 6 tablets). The tablets should be crushed to a powder and mixed in a teaspoon of cold water before being added to the sugar syrup. Fruit purée in particular is subject to darkening since large amounts of air are forced through a sieve during preparation. Air reacts on the cells of fruit to produce darkening; and for this reason fruit should be prepared quickly for freezing once the natural protection of skin or rind is broken. For the same reason, the fruit should be eaten immediately on thawing, or while a few ice crystals remain. Fruit which discolours badly is better for rapid thawing, and unsweetened frozen fruit should immediately be put into hot syrup or other liquid.

Jam Fruit

Any fruit can be packed for use in jam-making later. Pack without sweetening, and allow 10% extra fruit in the recipe when making the jam, as there is a slight pectin loss in frozen fruit.

Fruit Purée

It is useful to freeze purée for certain kinds of puddings and cakes, and when there is a lot of ripe fruit. The fruit should not be over-ripe or bruised. Raw fruit such as raspberries or strawberries should be sieved, to remove all the pips. Other fruit can be put in a covered dish in the oven to start the juice running before the fruit is sieved. Purée can be made from cooked fruit but must be well cooled before freezing (it will keep less than 4 months). This purée should be sweetened, as if for immediate use. Ways of preparing purée from individual fruits are given under the individual fruits below.

Fruit Syrups

Fruit syrups can be frozen; blackcurrant is thought best, and it is far easier to freeze than to bottle. Any standard syrup recipe can be used, and fruit syrup is best frozen in small quantities in ice-cube trays. Each cube should be wrapped in foil; then, a useful number of cubes are packed into a bag for storage. One syrup cube gives one individual serving to use with puddings or ice cream, or to dissolve in water as a drink.

Fruit Juices

Ripe fruit can be turned into juice, and frozen in this form. Citrus fruit juice can also be frozen. Non-citrus fruit should be carefully checked for any bruising or insects, then

Make this decorative flan with frozen apple slices in a frozen flan case and top with frozen apricots and prunes.

mashed with a silver fork. For every 4 cups of fruit, allow 1 cup of water and simmer gently for 10 minutes. Strain through a jelly bag or cloth, and cool completely before freezing. These juices can be frozen unsweetened, or sweetened to taste, and are useful for drinks, jellies and fruit pies. Freeze them in a rigid container, leaving $\frac{1}{2}$ in. headspace, or in ice-cube trays, wrapping each cube in foil and storing in quantities in polythene bags. Apple juice can be made, using $\frac{1}{2}$ pint water to each 2 lb. apples, or it can be made by simmering leftover peelings in water; it should *not* be sweetened before freezing since fermentation sets in quickly.

Citrus fruit juices can easily be prepared from good-quality fruit which is heavy in the hand for its size. The unpeeled fruit should be chilled in iced water or in the refrigerator before the juice is extracted; the juice can be strained, but the fine pulp can be left in if preferred. Freeze in rigid containers, leaving 1 in. headspace. Lemon and lime juice can usefully be frozen in ice-cube trays for drinks, the cubes being wrapped in foil and stored in useful quantities in polythene bags.

Catering Packs of Fruit and Juice
Large tins of fruit in syrup and of fruit juices are often economical to buy. They can be opened and divided into normal family portions, and then be frozen in smaller containers.

Thawing Frozen Fruit

Unsweetened fruit packs take longer to thaw than sweetened ones; fruit in dry sugar thaws most quickly of all. All fruit should be thawed in its container unopened; and all fruit is at its best when just thawed, with a few ice crystals left if it is to be eaten raw. Fruit to use with ice cream should only be partly defrosted. To cook frozen fruit, thaw until pieces can just be separated and put into a pie; if fruit is to be cooked in a saucepan, it can be put into the pan in its frozen state, keeping in mind the amount of sugar or syrup used earlier in freezing if a pudding is being made. Frozen fruits are likely to have a lot of juice after thawing; to avoid leaky pies or damp cake fillings, add a little thickening for pies (such as cornflour, arrowroot or flake tapioca), or drain off excess juice. For every 1 lb. fruit packed in syrup, allow 6–8 hours thawing time in the refrigerator, 2–4 hours thawing at room temperature, or ½–1 hour if the pack is placed in a bowl of cold water.

Fruit will lose quality and flavour if left to stand for any length of time after thawing, so do not thaw more than you need immediately. However, if leftover fruit is cooked, it will last for several days in a refrigerator.

Here are notes on preparing, packing, storing and cooking various fruits:

Apples

Preparation Peel, core and drop in cold water. Cut in twelfths or sixteenths. Pack in bags or boxes. (a) Dry sugar pack (8 oz sugar to 2 lb. fruit). (b) 40% syrup pack. (c) Sweetened purée.

Serving (a) Use for pies and puddings. (c) Use for sauce, fools and ices.
High Quality Storage Life (a) 8–12 months, (c) 4–8 months

Apricots

Preparation (a) Peeled and halved in dry sugar pack (4 oz sugar to 1 lb. fruit) or 40% syrup pack. (b) Peeled and sliced in 40% syrup pack. (c) Sweetened purée (very ripe fruit).

Serving (a) Thaw 3½ hours at room temperature. (b) Use for sauce, and ices.
High Quality Storage Life (a) 12 months, (c) 4 months

Avocado Pears

Preparation (a) Rub halves in lemon juice, wrap in foil and pack in polythene bags. (b) Dip slices in lemon juice and freeze in boxes. (c) Mash pulp with lemon juice (1 tablespoon to 1 avocado) and pack in small containers.

Serving (a) Thaw 2½ to 3 hours at room temperature and use at once. (b) Season pulp with onion, garlic or herbs as a spread.
High Quality Storage Life 2 months

53

Bananas

Preparation Mash with sugar and lemon juice (8 oz sugar to 3 tablespoons lemon juice to 3 breakfastcups banana pulp). Pack in small containers.

Serving Thaw 6 hours in unopened container in refrigerator. Use in sandwiches or cakes.
High Quality Storage Life 2 months

Blackberries

Preparation Wash dark glossy ripe berries and dry well. (a) Fast-freeze unsweetened berries on trays and pack in bags. (b) Dry sugar pack (8 oz sugar to 2 lb. fruit). (c) Sweetened purée (raw or cooked fruit).

Serving Thaw 3 hours at room temperature. Use raw, cooked or in pies and puddings.
High Quality Storage Life 12 months

Blueberries

Preparation Wash in chilled water and drain thoroughly. Crush fruit slightly as skins toughen on freezing. (a) Fast-freeze unsweetened berries on trays and pack in bags. (b) Dry sugar pack (4 oz sugar to 4 breakfastcups crushed berries). (c) 50% syrup pack.

Serving Use raw, cooked or in pies and puddings.
High Quality Storage Life 12 months

Cherries

Preparation Put in chilled water for 1 hour; remove stones. Pack in glass or plastic containers, as cherry juice remains liquid and leaks through waxed containers. (a) Dry sugar pack (8 oz sugar to 2 lb. stoned cherries). (b) 40% syrup pack for sweet cherries. (c) 50% or 60% syrup pack for sour cherries.

Serving Thaw 3 hours at room temperature. Serve cold, or use for pies.
High Quality Storage Life 12 months

Coconut

Preparation Grate or shred, moisten with coconut milk, and pack into bags or boxes; 4 oz sugar to 4 breakfastcups shredded coconut may be added if liked.

Serving Thaw 2 hours at room temperature. Drain off milk. Use for fruit salads, icings or curries.
High Quality Storage Life 2 months

Cranberries

Preparation Wash firm glossy berries and drain. (a) Dry unsweetened pack. (b) Sweetened purée.

Serving Cook in water and sugar while still frozen. Can be thawed $3\frac{1}{2}$ hours at room temperature.
High Quality Storage Life 12 months

Currants, Black, Red and White

Preparation Prepare black, red or white currants by the same methods. Strip fruit from stems with a fork, wash in chilled water and dry gently. Currants can be fast-frozen on trays and the stalks stripped off before packing. This makes the job easier. (a) Dry unsweetened pack. (b) Dry sugar pack (8 oz sugar to 1 lb. currants). (c) 40% syrup pack. (d) Sweetened purée (particularly blackcurrants).

Serving (a) Thaw 45 minutes at room temperature. Use for jam, pies and puddings. (c) and (d) Use as sauce, or for drinks, ices or puddings.
High Quality Storage Life 12 months

Damsons

Preparation Wash in chilled water; cut in half and remove stones. (a) 50% syrup pack. (b) Sweetened purée.

Serving Thaw at room temperature for $2\frac{1}{2}$ hours. Use cold, or for pies or puddings.
High Quality Storage Life 12 months

Dates

Preparation (a) Wrap block dates in foil or polythene bags. (b) Remove stones from dessert dates; pack in bags or boxes.

Serving Thaw 30 minutes at room temperature. Serve as dessert, or use for cakes or puddings.
High Quality Storage Life 12 months

Figs

Preparation   Wash fresh sweet ripe figs in chilled water; remove stems. Do not bruise. (a) Peeled or unpeeled in dry unsweetened pack. (b) 30% syrup pack for peeled figs. (c) Wrap dried dessert figs in foil or polythene bags.

Serving   Thaw 1½ hours at room temperature. Eat raw or cooked in syrup.
High Quality Storage Life   12 months

Gooseberries

Preparation   Wash in chilled water and dry. For pies, freeze fully ripe fruit; for jam, fruit may be slightly under-ripe. (a) Dry unsweetened pack. (b) 40% syrup pack. (c) Sweetened purée.

Serving   (a) and (b) Thaw 2½ hours at room temperature. Fruit may be put into pies or cooked while still frozen. (c) Thaw 2½ hours at room temperature and use for fools, mousses or ices.
High Quality Storage Life   12 months

Grapefruit

Preparation   Peel; remove pith; cut into segments. (a) Dry sugar pack (8 oz sugar to 2 breakfastcups segments). (b) 50% syrup pack.

Serving   Thaw 2½ hours at room temperature.
High Quality Storage Life   12 months

Grapes

Preparation   Pack seedless varieties whole. Skin, seed other types. Pack in 30% syrup.

Serving   Thaw 2½ hours at room temperature.
High Quality Storage Life   12 months

Greengages

Preparation   Wash in chilled water and dry. Cut in half and remove stones. Pack in 40% syrup.

Serving   Thaw 2½ hours at room temperature.
High Quality Storage Life   12 months

Guavas

Preparation   (a) Wash fruit, cook in a little water, and purée. Pineapple juice gives better flavour than water. (b) Peel, halve and cook until tender, then pack in 30% syrup.

Serving   Thaw $1\frac{1}{2}$ hours at room temperature.
High Quality Storage Life   12 months

Kumquats

Preparation   (a) Wrap whole fruit in foil. (b) 50% syrup pack.

Serving   Thaw 2 hours at room temperature.
High Quality Storage Life   (a) 2 months, (b) 12 months

Lemons and Limes

Preparation   Peel fruit, cut in slices, and pack in 20% syrup

Serving   Thaw 1 hour at toom temperature.
High Quality Storage Life   12 months

Loganberries

Preparation   Wash berries and dry well. (a) Fast-freeze unsweetened berries on trays and pack in bags. (b) Dry sugar pack (8 oz sugar to 2 lb. fruit). (c) 50% syrup pack. (d) Sweetened puree (cooked fruit).

Serving   Thaw 3 hours at room temperature. Use particularly for ices and mousses.
High Quality Storage Life   12 months

Mangoes

Preparation   Peel ripe fruit, and pack in slices in 50% syrup. Add 1 tablespoonful lemon juice to each quart syrup.

Serving   Thaw $1\frac{1}{2}$ hours at room temperature.
High Quality Storage Life   12 months

Melons

Preparation   Cut into cubes or balls. Toss in lemon juice and pack in 30% syrup.

Serving   Thaw unopened in refrigerator. Serve while still frosty.
High Quality Storage Life   12 months

Nectarines

Preparation   Wipe fruit, and peel or not as desired. Cut in halves or slices and brush with lemon juice. (a) 40% syrup pack. (b) Sweetened purée (fresh fruit) with 1 tablespoonful lemon juice to each lb. fruit.

Serving   Thaw 3 hours in refrigerator.
High Quality Storage Life   12 months

Oranges

Preparation   Peel and divide into sections or cut into slices. (a) Dry sugar pack (8 oz sugar to 3 breakfastcups sections or slices). (b) 30% syrup. (c) Pack slices in slightly sweetened fresh orange juice.

Serving   Thaw $2\frac{1}{2}$ hours at room temperature.
High Quality Storage Life   12 months
Navel oranges become bitter in the freezer. Seville oranges may be frozen whole in their skins in polythene bags for marmalade.

Peaches

Preparation   Work quickly as fruit discolours. Peel, cut in halves or slices and brush with lemon juice. (a) 40% syrup pack. (b) Sweetened purée (fresh fruit) with 1 tablespoon lemon juice to each lb. fruit.

Serving   Thaw 3 hours in refrigerator.
High Quality Storage Life   12 months

Pears

Preparation   Pears should be ripe, but not over-ripe. They discolour quickly and do not retain their delicate flavour in the freezer. Peel and quarter fruit, remove cores, and dip pieces in lemon juice. Poach in 30% syrup for $1\frac{1}{2}$ minutes. Drain and cool. Pack in cold 30% syrup.

Serving   Thaw 3 hours at room temperature.
High Quality Storage Life   12 months

Persimmons

Preparation   (a) Wrap whole fruit in foil. (b) Peel and freeze in 50% syrup adding 1 dessertspoon lemon juice to each quart syrup. (c) Sweetened purée (fresh fruit).

Serving   Thaw 3 hours at room temperature. Use unpeeled raw fruit as soon as it has thawed or it will darken and lose flavour.
High Quality Storage Life   (a) 2 months, (b) 12 months

Pineapple

Preparation   Use fully-ripe and golden-yellow fruit. Peel fruit and cut into slices or chunks. (a) Dry unsweetened pack, with slices separated by paper or cellophane. (b) Dry sugar pack (4 oz sugar to 1 lb. fruit). (c) 30% syrup pack. (d) Crush fruit and mix 4 oz sugar to 2 breakfastcups fruit.

Serving   Thaw 3 hours at room temperature.
High Quality Storage Life   12 months

Plums

Preparation   Wash in chilled water and dry. Cut in half and remove stones. Pack in 40% syrup.

Serving   Thaw $2\frac{1}{2}$ hours at room temperature.
High Quality Storage Life   12 months

Pomegranates

Preparation   (a) Cut ripe fruit in half; scoop out juice sacs and pack in 50% syrup. (b) Extract juice and sweeten to taste. Freeze in ice cube trays, and wrap frozen cubes in foil for storage.

Serving   Thaw 3 hours at room temperature.
High Quality Storage Life   12 months

Quinces

Preparation   Peel, core and slice. Simmer in boiling 20% syrup for 20 minutes. Cool and pack in cold 20% syrup.

Serving   Thaw 3 hours at room temperature.
High Quality Storage Life   12 months

Raspberries

Preparation (a) Dry unsweetened pack. (b) Dry sugar pack (4 oz sugar to 1 lb. fruit). (c) 30% syrup. (d) Sweetened purée (fresh fruit).

Serving Thaw 3 hours at room temperature. Use purée as sauce, or for drinks, ices, or mousses.
High Quality Storage Life 12 months

Rhubarb

Preparation Wash sticks in cold running water, and trim to required length. (a) Blanch sticks 1 minute, then wrap in foil or polythene. (b) 40% syrup pack. (c) Sweetened purée (cooked fruit).

Serving Thaw 3 hours at room temperature. Raw fruit can be cooked while still frozen.
High Quality Storage Life 12 months

Strawberries

Preparation Use ripe, mature and firm fruit. Pick over fruit, removing hulls. (a) Grade for size in dry unsweetened pack. (b) Dry sugar pack (4 oz sugar to 1 lb. fruit). Fruit may be sliced or lightly crushed. (c) 40% syrup for whole or sliced fruit. (d) Sweetened purée (fresh fruit).

Serving Thaw 1½ hours at room temperature.
High Quality Storage Life 12 months

Frozen strawberries can be used to fill cream buns at any time of year.

Here are some useful fruit-based recipes for your freezer:

Apple Sauce

Apples
Sugar
Lemon juice

Slice the apples but do not peel them. Put them into a casserole with water barely to cover. Put on a lid and cook at 325°F, 170°C, Gas Mark 3, for 45 minutes until the apples are soft. Sieve the apples and sweeten to taste, adding a good squeeze of lemon juice. Cool and pack into small containers.

To serve
Thaw for 3 hours at room temperature.
High Quality Storage Life   1 year

Cranberry Sauce

1 lb cranberries
12 oz sugar
¾ pint water

Rinse the cranberries. Dissolve the sugar in water over a gentle heat. Add the cranberries and cook gently for 15 minutes until the cranberries burst. Cool and pack into small containers.

To serve
Thaw at room temperature for 3 hours.
High Quality Storage Life   1 year

Gooseberry Sauce

1 lb gooseberries
1 oz butter
*2 tablespoons caster
   sugar*

Wash gooseberries, but do not top and tail them. Put in a pan with 2 tablespoons water and the butter. Cover and cook 15 minutes on low heat until soft. Put through a sieve and then reheat purée with sugar until dissolved. Chill and pack in small containers.

To serve
Reheat gently and use with fish, or with steamed puddings.
High Quality Storage Life   3 months

Seville Orange Sauce (for duck or pork)

Wash the oranges and peel them very thinly. Cut the peel into match-stick strips, and boil it in a little water for 10 minutes until soft. Cool and mix with the strained juice of the oranges. Pack in small cartons to freeze. The juice and peel of 3 oranges will be enough for one joint or bird.

To serve
Thaw the juice, and take out and reserve the strips of peel. Baste the pork or duck with the juice. When the meat is done, pour off the surplus fat. Add a little white wine or stock to the pan juices and stir while heating. Stir in the peel strips just before serving.
High Quality Storage Life   1 year

Jam stored in the freezer retains a full fruit flavour and colour and is a good way of preserving surplus fruit. It is easy to make as no boiling or testing are required.

Strawberry Jam

$1\frac{1}{2}$ lb strawberries
2 lb caster sugar
4 fl. oz liquid pectin

Mash or sieve strawberries and stir with sugar in a bowl. Leave for 20 minutes, stirring occasionally, then add pectin and stir for 3 minutes. Pack in small waxed or rigid plastic containers, cover tightly and seal. Leave at room temperature for 24–48 hours until jelled before freezing.

To serve
Thaw at room temperature for 1 hour.
High Quality Storage Life   6 months

Apricot or Peach Jam

$1\frac{1}{2}$ lb ripe fresh apricots
   or peaches
2 lb caster sugar
4 fl. oz liquid pectin
1 teaspoon powdered
   citric acid

Skin apricots or peaches and remove stones. Mash fruit and stir in sugar and acid. Leave for 20 minutes, stirring occasionally, then add pectin and stir for 3 minutes. Pack in small waxed or rigid plastic containers, cover tightly and seal. Leave at room temperature for 24–48 hours until jelled before freezing.

To serve
Thaw at room temperature for 1 hour.
High Quality Storage Life   1 year

Lemon Curd

3 lemons or $\frac{1}{4}$ pint
   lemon juice
2 oz butter
12 oz caster sugar
3 eggs

Grate the rind of the lemons and squeeze out the juice. There should be about $\frac{1}{4}$ pint juice. Put the rind, juice, butter and sugar into the top of a double saucepan, or into a bowl over hot water. Heat gently until the butter melts and the sugar has dissolved. Add the lightly beaten eggs and stir constantly over low heat until the mixture becomes thick. Do not boil. Cool and put into small freezer cartons.

To serve
Thaw at room temperature for 3 hours.
High Quality Storage Life   6 months

Orange Sorbet

2 teaspoons gelatine
½ pint water
6 oz sugar
1 teaspoon grated lemon
    rind
1 teaspoon grated
    orange rind
½ pint orange juice
4 tablespoons lemon
    juice
2 egg whites

Soak gelatine in a little of the water and boil the rest of the water and sugar for 10 minutes to a syrup. Stir gelatine into syrup and cool. Add rinds and juices. Beat egg whites stiff but not dry, and fold into mixture. Freeze to a mush, beat once, then continue freezing allowing 3 hours total freezing time. This ice will not go completely hard. Pack into containers, cover, seal, label and store in freezer. For party occasions, this ice may be packed into fresh fruit containers. Scoop out oranges or lemons, wash them and fill with sorbet. Pack into containers, seal, label and store in freezer. If the ice has not been prepacked into fruit cases, the containers may be prepared before serving. To do this, scoop out oranges and lemons, wash and put into freezer wet so that they get a frosted surface. Thirty minutes before serving, scoop out the ice from its large container into the cases and leave in the freezer until serving time. The same recipe may be used for a lemon sorbet, using only lemon juice and rind instead of a mixture of orange and lemon.

Viennese Red Currant Ice

1 lb redcurrants
4 oz redcurrant jelly
1 pint water
1 large ripe tomato
4 oz raspberries
Juice and rind of
    ½ lemon
3 oz caster sugar
Red vegetable colouring
4 egg yolks
2 tablespoons white rum
    or brandy
½ pint double cream

Remove currants from stalks and simmer with redcurrant jelly, hot water, tomato, raspberries, juice and rind of lemon, sugar and colouring until the fruit is a pulp. Cool and add well-beaten egg yolks and rum or brandy. Rub through a sieve, and freeze to a batter. Add whipped cream and continue freezing for 2 hours. Pick into waxed or rigid plastic containers.

To serve
Scoop into glasses.
High Quality Storage Life   2 months

Spiced Apples

8 oz sugar
¾ pint water
4 in. cinnamon stick
6 firm eating apples
Pink colouring

Put the sugar, water and cinnamon stick into a saucepan and heat until the sugar dissolves. Peel and core the apples and cut into ¼ in. rings. Simmer a few apple rings at a time until just tender, adding a little colouring to syrup for a better appearance. Take the slices from the syrup, drain and cool. Arrange slices on a baking sheet and freeze. Pack the slices in freezer foil or small containers. Remove the cinnamon from the syrup and freeze in small containers.

To serve
Thaw at room temperature for 1 hour, and serve round pork, ham or goose. Use the syrup for making apple sauce, or for adding to pies.
High Quality Storage Life   2 months

Fruit fritters, here made with apple rings.

Fruit Fritters

4 oz plain flour
Pinch of salt
1 egg and 1 egg yolk
½ pint milk
6 eating apples or 6 bananas or 1 large can pineapple rings
1 tablespoon melted butter
1 tablespoon fresh white breadcrumbs

Prepare batter by mixing together flour, salt, egg and egg yolk and milk, and folding in melted butter and breadcrumbs. Peel, core and slice apples into ¼-in. rings, or cut bananas in half lengthways. Dip fruit into batter and fry until golden in deep fat. Drain on absorbent paper and cool. Pack in polythene bags, foil or waxed containers, separating fritters with Cellophane or waxed paper.

To serve
Put in a single layer on baking tray, thaw and heat at 375°F, 190°C, Gas Mark 5, for 10 minutes. Toss in sugar before serving.
High Quality Storage Life 1 month

Stuffed Peaches

8 large ripe peaches
4 oz ground almonds
3 oz icing sugar
1½ oz butter
Grated rind of 1 lemon
1 tablespoon orange juice
4 tablespoons sherry

Peel peaches and cut in halves. Mix ground almonds with icing sugar, soft butter and lemon rind and work in orange juice to give a soft paste. Form paste into eight small balls. Put peaches together round stuffing and put on oven dish. Pour on sherry and sprinkle thickly with icing sugar. Bake at 400°F, 200°C, Gas Mark 6, for 15 minutes and cool quickly. Pack in individual containers, or by covering container in which peaches have been cooked in foil.

To serve
Thaw at room temperature for 2 hours, uncover and heat at 375°F, 190°C, Gas Mark 5, for 10 minutes. Serve with cream.
High Quality Storage Life 1 month

Fruit crumble made with sliced peaches.

Fruit Crumble

*1 lb apples, plums or
  rhubarb
6 oz plain flour
3 oz brown sugar
4 oz butter or margarine*

Clean and prepare fruit by peeling and/or slicing and arrange in greased pie dish or foil container, sweetening to taste (about 3 oz sugar to 1 lb. fruit). Prepare topping by rubbing fat into flour and sugar until mixture is like breadcrumbs. Sprinkle topping on fruit and press down. Pack the fruit crumble uncooked by covering with heavy duty foil, or by putting container into polythene bag.

To serve
Put container into cold oven and cook at 400°F, 200°C, Gas Mark 6, for 30 minutes, then at 375°F, 190°C, Gas Mark 5, for 45 minutes.
High Quality Storage Life 6 months (apples may discolour; a little lemon juice will help to prevent this).

65

Swedish Applecake

*3 oz fresh brown
  breadcrumbs
1 oz butter
2 tablespoons brown
  sugar
1 lb apples*

Gently fry breadcrumbs in butter until golden brown. Cook apples in very little water until soft, and sweeten to taste. Stir brown sugar into buttered crumbs and arrange alternate layers of buttered crumbs and apples in buttered dish, beginning and ending with a layer of crumbs. Press firmly into dish and cool. Pack by covering with foil lid.

To serve
Thaw without lid in refrigerator for 1 hour, turn out and serve with cream.
High Quality Storage Life   1 month

Pears in Red Wine

*8 eating pears
8 oz sugar
$\frac{1}{4}$ pint water
$\frac{1}{4}$ pint Burgundy
2-in. cinnamon stick*

Peel pears but leave whole with stalks on. Dissolve sugar in water and add cinnamon stick. Simmer pears in syrup with lid on for 15 minutes, then add burgundy and uncover the pan. Continue simmering for 15 minutes. Drain pears and put into individual leakproof containers. Reduce syrup by boiling until it is thick, then pour over pears, and cool. Pack into leakproof containers since the syrup does not freeze solid; the pears lose moisture on thawing and thin the syrup, but the effect is lessened if they are packed in individual containers.

To serve
Thaw in refrigerator for 8 hours.
High Quality Storage Life   2 months

Fruit Cream

*1 lb raspberries,
  currants,
  gooseberries or
  blackberries
$\frac{3}{4}$ pint water
6 oz sugar
2 tablespoons cornflour*

Clean fruit. Bring water to boil, add fruit and sugar, and boil until fruit is soft. Mix cornflour with a little cold water, blend into hot liquid, and bring back to boil. Cool. Pack in serving dish covered with foil.

To serve
Thaw in refrigerator for 1 hour and serve with cream.
High Quality Storage Life   1 month

Fruit Mousse

*$\frac{1}{4}$ pint fruit purée
1 oz caster sugar
$\frac{1}{4}$ pint double cream
2 egg whites
Juice of $\frac{1}{2}$ lemon*

Mix fruit purée and sugar. Whip cream lightly, and whip egg whites stiffly. Add lemon juice to fruit, then fold in cream and egg white. A little colouring may be added if the fruit is pale. Pack in serving dish covered with foil.

To serve
Thaw in refrigerator without lid for 2 hours.
High Quality Storage Life   1 month

FREEZING MEAT

Both raw and cooked meat usually store extremely well in the freezer. But it is important to choose high-quality raw meat for storage, whether fresh or frozen, since freezing does not improve poor meat in either texture or flavour (although tender meat may become a little more tender in storage).

Many authorities feel that fresh meat should not be frozen in domestic freezers, since it is not possible to achieve the very low temperatures thought necessary for successful freezing. This point should be thought about carefully when buying in bulk for the freezer. It is also important not to overload the freezer with bulky quantities of meat at the expense of other items, and to keep a good regular turnover of supplies. One good compromise is to use the freezer for keeping special high quality cuts, or those which are not often obtainable, such as pork fillet, veal and fillet steak, together with a variety of prepared dishes made from the cheaper cuts which are useful when time is likely to be short for food preparation. Fresh meat must be hung for the required time before freezing.

Choosing Meat for the Freezer

Meat should be chosen with the family needs in mind. The better cuts are bound to be more popular, but bulk buying will be a false economy if the family does not eat the cheaper cuts at all. Meat must be of good quality whatever the cut, and must be properly hung (beef 8–12 days; lamb 5–7 days; pork and veal chilled only). Before buying bulk meat, check the diagrams given and suggested uses for each part of the animal, and see if this will fit into the family eating plan.

Beef	THE BETTER CUTS	SUGGESTED USES
	Sirloin	Roasting, preferably on the bone Grilling as Sirloin Steak Entrecôte Steak Porterhouse Steak T-bone Steak
	Fillet	Roasting in pastry case Grilling as Châteaubriand Fillet Steak Tournedos (trimmed)
	Rump Steak	Roasting in the piece Grilling

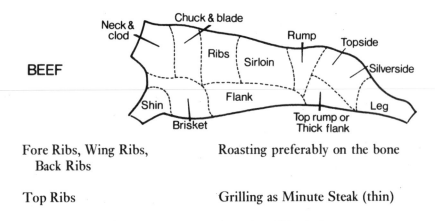

BEEF

Fore Ribs, Wing Ribs, Back Ribs	Roasting preferably on the bone
Top Ribs	Grilling as Minute Steak (thin)
Topside	Roasting, if larded
	Pot Roasting

THE ECONOMY CUTS

Top Rump or Thick Flank	Pot Roasting
Flank	Pot Roasting (if boned and rolled)
Brisket	Slow Roasting (if de-fatted and rolled)
	Pot Roasting
Silverside	Pot Roasting
Shin	Stewing
	Stock
Leg	Stewing
	Stock
Neck and Clod	Stewing
	Stock
Chuck and Blade	Stewing
	Pies and Puddings
Skirt	Stewing
	Pies and Puddings

Lamb and Mutton	**THE BETTER CUTS**	**SUGGESTED USES**
	Saddle (Double Loin)	Roasting
	Loin	Roasting (on or off bone)
		Chops
	Leg (Fillet End and Knuckle End)	Roasting
		Boiling

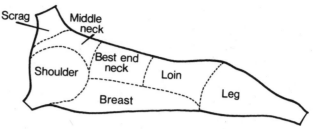

LAMB

Shoulder (Blade End and Knuckle End)	Roasting (on or off bone)

THE ECONOMY CUTS

Best End of Neck	Roasting (chined, and as Crown of Lamb)
	Cutlets
	Stewing
Middle Neck	Stewing
Scrag End of Neck	Stewing
Breast of Lamb	Roasting (boned, stuffed and rolled)
	Stewing

Pork

THE BETTER CUTS	**SUGGESTED USES**
Leg	Roasting (on or off bone)
Loin	Roasting (on or off bone)
	Chops

THE ECONOMY CUTS

Blade	Roasting

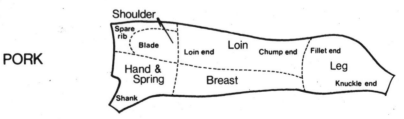

PORK

Spare Rib	Roasting
Hand and Spring	Roasting (boned, stuffed and rolled)
Belly	Roasting (boned)
	Grilling (slices)
	Pâté

High quality and economy cuts chosen for the freezer: the roast joint and steaks (left) come from the top quality range, while the chopped meat is made from economy cuts.

Preparation for Freezing Meat

Bulk supplies of meat should be packaged in quantities which can be used up on a single occasion if possible. Ideally, meat should be boned and the surplus fat removed so as not to take up unnecessary freezer space; if the bones are *not* removed, the ends should be wrapped in several layers of greaseproof paper to avoid piercing freezer wrappings. Meat must be carefully labelled for identification, as identification may be difficult otherwise. Air must be excluded from the packages so that the freezer wrap can touch the surface of the meat all over.

If a whole animal or a variety of different meats are being prepared for freezing at one time, the offal should be processed first, then pork, veal and lamb, and finally beef as this will keep best under refrigeration if delays occur. Normally, not more than 4 lb. of meat per cubic foot of freezer space should be frozen at one time for good results.

The wrapping for meat must be strong, since oxygen from the air which may penetrate wrappings affects fat and may cause rancidity (pork is the most subject to this problem). In addition to moisture-vapour-proof wrapping, an overwrap of brown paper, greaseproof paper or stockinette will protect packages and will guard against punctures from projecting bones or other packets; place the label on the outside of this wrapping. It is worth taking this precaution, since meat is likely to be the most costly item stored in the freezer.

70

Cooking Frozen Meat

Frozen meat can be cooked when thawed or unthawed, but partial or complete thawing helps it to retain its juiciness. Thin cuts of meat and minced meat may toughen if cooked while still frozen. Offal must always be completely thawed. All meat should be thawed in its wrapping, and preferably in a refrigerator since slow thawing is required. Allow 5 hours per lb. in a refrigerator and 2 hours per lb. at room temperature. If it is really necessary to hurry thawing, this can be done in a cool oven (200° F, 100° C or Gas Mark $\frac{1}{4}$) allowing 25 minutes per lb. but the meat's flavour will not be so good. If meat must be cooked from the frozen state, unthawed large cuts will take $1\frac{1}{2}$ times as long as fresh ones; smaller thin cuts will take $1\frac{1}{4}$ times as long. When thawing offal, sausages and mince, allow $1\frac{1}{2}$ hours at room temperature or 3 hours in a refrigerator for 1 lb. of meat.

Frozen meat can be roasted, braised, grilled, fried or stewed in the same way as fresh meat. In any roasting process, however, it is best to use a slow oven method (for beef, use 300° F, 150° C or Gas Mark 2, and also for lamb; for pork use 350° F, 180° C or Gas Mark 4). Chops and steaks will cook while still frozen if put into a thick frying pan just rubbed with fat and cooked very gently for the first 5 minutes on each side, then browned more quickly. Meat should be cooked as soon as it is thawed, and still cold, to prevent loss of juices.

Here are notes on preparing, packing, storing and cooking various kinds of meat:

Casseroles and Stews

Preparation Use a standard recipe, but slightly undercook vegetables. Do not add potatoes, rice or pasta. Thicken with cornflour if necessary. Cool completely and remove surplus fat. Pack in boxes or in foil-lined casserole, making sure meat is covered with liquid. When frozen, remove foil package from casserole for storage.

Serving Heat in double boiler or in oven at 350°F, 180°C, Gas Mark 4 for 45 minutes.
High Quality Storage Life 2 months

Meat casseroles can be topped with sliced potatoes before cooking and freezing.

Cubed Meat

Preparation Package in usable quantities. Trim fat and cut meat into neat pieces. Press tightly into bags or boxes, removing air.

Serving Thaw in wrappings in refrigerator for 3 hours ($1\frac{1}{2}$ hours at room temperature).
High Quality Storage Life 2 months

Ham

Preparation Package in the piece rather than sliced. Pack in freezer paper, foil or polythene, and overwrap. Vacuum-packed bacon may be frozen in its packing. Storage life is limited as salt causes rancidity.

Serving Thaw in wrappings in refrigerator.
High Quality Storage Life 3 months (whole); 1 month (sliced)

Hearts, Kidneys, Sweetbreads, Tongue

Preparation Wash and dry thoroughly. Remove blood vessels and pipes. Wrap in cellophane or polythene and pack in bags or boxes. Off-flavours may develop if offal is not packed with care.

Serving Thaw in wrappings in refrigerator for 3 hours ($1\frac{1}{2}$ hours at room temperature.
High Quality Storage Life 2 months

Joints

Preparation Trim surplus fat. Bone and roll if possible. Pad sharp bones. Wipe meat. Pack in polythene bag or sheeting, freezer paper or foil. Remove air. Freeze quickly.

Serving Thaw in wrappings in refrigerator, allow 5 hours per lb. Roast by slow-oven method (300°F, 150°C or Gas Mark 2 for beef and lamb; 350°F, 130°C or Gas Mark 4 for pork).
High Quality Storage Life Beef 12 months; Lamb 9 months; Pork 6 months; Veal 9 months.

Liver

Preparation Package whole or in slices. Separate slices with greaseproof paper or cellophane.

Serving Thaw in wrappings in refrigerator for 3 hours ($1\frac{1}{2}$ hours at room temperature).
High Quality Storage Life 2 months

Meat (Cooked)

Preparation Avoid freezing whole cooked joints, steaks or chops, and fried meats, which tend to toughness, dryness and rancidity when frozen. (a) Slice cooked meat in $\frac{1}{4}$ in. slices and separate with greaseproof paper or Cellophane. Pack tightly in boxes or foil dishes with lids. (b) Slice meat and pack in gravy or sauce, which should be thickened with cornflour rather than flour. Pack in foil dishes with lids.

Serving (a) Thaw in wrappings in refrigerator for 3 hours. Separate slices and dry on absorbent paper. (b) Heat in container at 350°F, 120°C, Gas Mark 4 for 30 minutes.
High Quality Storage Life 2 months

Meat Pies

Preparation (a) Prepare and cook pie in foil container. Before filling, brush bottom crust with melted fat to prevent sogginess. Cool and wrap in foil or in polythene bag. (b) Prepare and cook meat filling. Put into foil container and cover with fresh pastry. Wrap in foil or in polythene bag.

Serving (a) Thaw in refrigerator for 6 hours to serve cold. Heat at 375°F, 190°C, Gas Mark 5 for 1 hour to serve hot. (b) Remove wrappings. Bake at 400°F, 200°C, Gas Mark 6 for 1 hour.
High Quality Storage Life 2 months

Minced Meat

Preparation (a) Use good quality mince without fat. Pack in bags or boxes. Do not add salt. Remove air. Freeze quickly. (b) Shape mince into patties, separated, and pack in bags or boxes. Remove air. Freeze quickly.

Serving Thaw in wrappings in refrigerator for 3 hours ($1\frac{1}{2}$ hours at room temperature). Can be used while frozen, but may be tough.
High Quality Storage Life 2 months

Sausages and Sausage Meat

Preparation Omit salt in preparation. Pack in usable quantities. Wrap tightly in freezer paper, foil or polythene.

Serving Thaw in wrappings in refrigerator for 2 hours. Sausages can be cooked while frozen.
High Quality Storage Life 1 month

Sausages, cooked while still frozen and used to top a thawed fruit purée (p. 51).

Steaks and Chops

Preparation   Package in usable quantities. Separate pieces of meat with greaseproof paper or cellophane. Pack in polythene bag or sheeting, freezer paper or foil. Remove air. Freeze quickly.

Serving   Thaw in wrappings in refrigerator or use while frozen. Cook gently on both sides in a lightly-oiled thick pan. Brown to serve.
High Quality Storage Life   6–12 months (according to type of meat)

Tripe

Preparation   Cut in 1 in. squares and pack tightly in bags or boxes.

Serving   Thaw in wrappings in refrigerator for 3 hours (1½ hours at room temperature).
High Quality Storage Life   2 months

Lamb chops cooked while still frozen.

Meat Pudding

Preparation (a) Prepare pudding with suet crust to standard recipe. Cook in foil or polythene basin and cool quickly. Wrap tightly in foil. (b) Cook meat filling and pack in foil or polythene basins for freezing.

Serving Remove wrapping. Cover pastry with foil and cook frozen pudding for 3 hours. (b) Remove lids. Cover with fresh suet pastry, cook 3 hours.
High Quality Storage Life 2 months

Shepherd's Pie

Preparation Make from fresh or cooked meat, using plenty of stock or gravy to keep moist. Cool meat completely and put into foil container. Prepare mashed potatoes and cool completely. Spread on meat. Cover with foil or pack in polythene bag.

Serving Bake at 400°F, 200°C, Gas Mark 6 for 45 minutes until potatoes are golden.
High Quality Storage Life 2 months

Braised Beef

1 lb mixed vegetables (carrots, onions, celery, leeks, turnips)
3 lb rolled rib beef
2 oz lard or dripping
Salt and pepper
Parsley, thyme and bay leaf
Water or stock

Peel vegetables and cut into neat cubes to make a layer 2 in. thick in a pan which will just fit the beef. Fry the meat in the fat until browned on all sides, and put on top of the vegetables. Add seasoning and herbs, and pour in hot water or stock to a depth of about 1 in. Cover and cook at 325°F, 170°C, Gas Mark 3, for 1½ hours. Cool. Pack in foil or rigid plastic container.

To serve
Return to casserole and heat at 325°F, 170°C, Gas Mark 3, for 1 hour.
High Quality Storage Life 2 months

Pot Roast Beef with Vegetables

2 lb flank beef (chined and tied into round shape)
2 carrots
1 turnip
1 onion
Good ⅛th pint stock
Salt and pepper
Thyme, parsley and bayleaf
Dripping

Heat dripping in pan until smoking hot and brown meat on all sides. Place chopped vegetables round the meat and add the seasoning and herbs. Pour over the stock. Cover pan with a tight-fitting lid. Simmer gently until meat is tender, about 2 hours. Pack and freeze.

To serve
Reheat in a covered dish at 325°F, 170°C, Gas Mark 3, for 1¼ hours.
High Quality Storage Life 2 months

Sweet and Sour Lamb can make the basis of a Chinese meal from the freezer.

Jellied Beef

4 lb beef brisket
8 oz lean bacon
Salt and pepper
1 pint red wine
2 oz butter
2 oz oil
½ pint stock
Pinch of nutmeg
Parsley, thyme and
  bayleaf
4 onions
4 carrots
1 calf's foot

Use beef which has not too much fat and see that it is firmly tied. Soak in wine for 2 hours after rubbing all over with salt and pepper. Drain meat and then brown all over in a mixture of butter and oil, together with the chopped bacon. Put in casserole with the wine, stock, nutmeg, herbs, onions, carrots and split calf's foot. Cover and cook at 325°F, 170°C, Gas Mark 3, for 3 hours. Cool slightly and slice beef and put into containers with sliced vegetables. Strain liquid and cool, pour over, cover and freeze.

To serve
Thaw in refrigerator to eat cold, or heat in covered dish at 350°F, 180°C, Gas Mark 4, for 45 minutes.
High Quality Storage Life 2 months

Sweet and Sour Lamb

1 boned breast of lamb
  (1½ lb)
1 sliced onion
1 sliced carrot
½ pint stock
2 dessertspoons vinegar
1 dessertspoon cornflour
1 dessertspoon soya
  sauce
1 dessertspoon brown
  sugar

Cut breast into thin strips. Fry in own fat until crisp. Drain. Blend cornflour and add all the other ingredients. Add the lamb and simmer for an hour. Cool, pack in foil container and freeze.

To serve
Reheat gently in double boiler and serve with rice or noodles, and with a green vegetable in the dish if desired.
High Quality Storage Life 1 month

Pot-Roasted Stuffed Shoulder of Lamb

2 lb shoulder lamb
2 onions
½ parsnip
2 sticks celery
2 carrots
Salt and pepper
Thyme, parsley and
   bayleaf
Dripping

Stuffing
6 oz pork sausagemeat
8-oz can apricots
2 oz breadcrumbs
Salt and pepper

Have the lamb boned. Chop all the vegetables. Mix all stuffing ingredients together in a bowl. Put stuffing into lamb, and tie into a round shape. Heat dripping in frying pan and brown meat on all sides. Place in a saucepan and surround meat with vegetables. Add seasoning and herbs and cover with tight-fitting lid. Cook slowly on top of the stove until meat is tender. The meat may also be cooked in a casserole at 325°F, 170°C, Gas Mark 3, for 2½ hours. Pack and freeze.

To serve
Reheat in a covered dish at 325°F, 170°C, Gas Mark 3, for 1¼ hours.
High Quality Storage Life 2 months

Braised Pork and Tomatoes

2 lb hand or shoulder of
  pork
2 oz lard
2 chopped onions
6 tomatoes, skinned and
  sliced
Salt and pepper
¼ pint dry cider

Heat lard in frying pan and brown meat on all sides. Remove the meat. Fry the onions for a few minutes, then add tomatoes and seasoning and toss in the fat to coat. Place vegetables in a casserole, place the meat on the vegetables and pour the cider over. Place in oven and cook at 170° C (325° F) Gas Mark 3 for 1½ hours. When cooked, slice meat and surround with the braised vegetables. Pack in foil dish, cover and freeze.

To serve
Reheat at 180° C (350° F) Gas Mark 4 for 45 minutes.
High Quality Storage Life   1 month

Mushroom and Beefburger Risotto

1½ oz butter
1 large onion
6 oz sliced button
  mushrooms
8 oz long grain rice
1½ pints beef stock
2 teaspoons
  Worcestershire sauce
12 frozen beefburgers
6 oz frozen peas
Salt and pepper
Tomato wedges for
  garnish

Melt butter in large saucepan and fry onion for 3 minutes. Add mushrooms and cook for 1 minute. Add rice and cook gently for 1 minute stirring. Add stock and Worcestershire sauce, bring to boil, cover and simmer for 15 minutes. Cook beefburgers according to pack instructions, cut into quarters and add to risotto with peas. Cook for further 5 minutes until liquid is absorbed. Serve hot garnished with tomato wedges.

79

Cornish pasties.

Beefburger Kebabs

8 quartered frozen
    beefburgers
4 oz blanched button
    mushrooms
8 small tomatoes
8 pickled onions
1 tablespoon cooking oil
Watercress sprigs to
    garnish

Arrange quarters of beefburgers on 8 skewers alternately with vegetables. Brush with oil and cook under a moderately hot grill for about 5 minutes, turning frequently, until cooked.

Cornish Pasties

1 lb plain flour
1 teaspoon salt
6 oz lard
4 tablespoons finely
    grated suet
Water to mix
2 large potatoes
1 small turnip
1 onion
12 oz lean chopped
    chuck steak
Salt and pepper

Mix the flour and salt, rub in the lard and add the suet. Mix to a stiff paste with water, and roll out to ¼-in. thickness. Cut into six rounds, using a 6½-in. plate to cut the size. Slice the potatoes, turnip and onion finely, and place a mixture down the centre of each round, seasoning well. On top put the chopped meat. Damp the edge of each round, and close each pasty across the top, sealing the edges firmly. Pinch the edges between finger and thumb to give a fluted top. Put on a baking sheet and bake in a very hot oven, 450° F (230° C) Gas Mark 8 for 10 minutes. Reduce heat to moderate, 350° F (180° C) Gas Mark 4 and continue cooking until the meat is tender (about 45 minutes). Cool and freeze in polythene bag.

To serve
Heat at 325°F (170°C) Gas Mark 3 for 45 minutes, or thaw and serve cold.
High Quality Storage Life 2 months.

Savoury Pie

12 oz minced belly pork
1 large onion
2 tomatoes
1 dessertspoon curry
    powder
Salt and pepper
1 lb mashed potatoes
1 oz lard
Little melted butter

Melt lard and fry curry powder for 2 minutes. Add finely chopped onion and meat, and fry for 5 minutes. Add peeled and chopped tomatoes and seasoning. Turn into a pie dish and cover with mashed potatoes. Brush over with melted butter. Bake in oven for 20 minutes at 400°F, 200°C, Gas Mark 6. Cover and freeze.

To serve
Reheat at 325°F, 170°C, Gas Mark 3, for 1 hour.
High Quality Storage Life   2 months

Potato Hot Dogs

6 even-sized old potatoes
6 frozen skinless pork
    sausages
5 oz carton sour cream
2 tablespoons chopped
    chives or spring onions

Scrub potatoes well, dry and prick with a fork. Bake at 190° C (375° F) Gas Mark 5 for about 1 hour until cooked. Grill or fry sausages until cooked and keep warm. Cut potatoes in half lengthways, keeping the 2 halves attached at one side. Cut sausages in half, place in potato and spoon over soured cream mixed with chives. Serve hot.

Meat Loaf

2 lb beef mince
1 lb minced pie veal
1 lb pork mince
3 finely chopped onions
2 carrots
2 crushed garlic cloves
$\frac{1}{4}$ pint milk
4 oz breadcrumbs
1 teaspoon salt
2 crushed bayleaves
2 teaspoons Tabasco
   sauce
$\frac{1}{2}$ teaspoon thyme
$\frac{1}{2}$ teaspoon allspice
2 eggs

Combine all the ingredients for the loaf together in a large bowl and mix well. Press firmly into a greased baking tin approx. $12 \times 8 \times 1\frac{1}{4}$ in. or into 2 tins. Bake at 350°F, 180°C, Gas Mark 4, for $1\frac{1}{4}$ hours. Cool and pack in foil or polythene for freezing.

To serve
Reheat or serve cold with a spicy tomato sauce.
High Quality Storage Life   2 months

FREEZING BACON

Buying Bacon for Freezing

(a) Freshness of the bacon is the first vital step to successful freezing. Try and get the bacon the day that the retailer gets delivery from his supplier.

(b) Determine storage period in relation to freshness, and reduce the recommended period if in doubt.

(c) Smoked bacon can be stored for longer than unsmoked bacon.

(d) The quicker bacon is frozen right through, the better it will be. It is therefore inadvisable to freeze pieces weighing more than 5 lb.

Preparing Bacon for Freezing

(a) **Freshly-cut bacon joints.** (i) Determine the size of joint to be required for each meal and cut to this size; (ii) wrap each piece in foil, allowing ample covering; (iii) exclude as much air as possible; (iv) place each parcel of bacon into a polythene bag. The thicker the bag the better; (v) again exclude as much air as possible. Clip or tie the bag immediately; (vi) mark date and content on each packet.

(b) **Bacon rashers, chops and steaks.** It may be necessary to freeze these small pieces of bacon but storage time is much less than for joints, only 2 to 4 weeks. This is because so much of the meat and fat surface has been exposed to air with risk of rancidity developing. It is more practical to buy vacuum packed bacon which can be stored in a refrigerator for the same periods. $\frac{1}{2}$ lb. packets which can be thawed and eaten promptly are recommended. If freezing, say before going away on holiday, follow packing instructions for bacon joints.

Freezing Vacuum Packed Bacon

Vacuum packing of bacon is the ideal preparation for storage in the freezer because air has already been withdrawn from the packet. Vacuum packing is a commercial process and cannot be undertaken at home. Vacuum packed rashers and joints are almost always available in all shops.

A lot of vacuum packed bacon is so marked; but as vacuum-packing can be confused with other types of wrappings, it is advisable to check this if one is in doubt.

To prepare these packets for the freezer, inspect each one to ensure the vacuum is not damaged, i.e. the bacon should not be loose in the packet. Wrap the packets in foil, and label.

Freezer-stored bacon chops
after thawing and cooking.

Thawing Frozen Bacon

(a) Joints. Allow bacon plenty of time to thaw slowly, preferably in a refrigerator. Bacon can be thawed at room temperature before cooking. Time required depends on the thickness of the piece and the temperature. The wrapping should be removed as soon as possible during thawing.

(b) Bacon rashers and small pieces may be thawed overnight in the refrigerator or dipped in hot water for a few minutes until soft. Dry on kitchen paper before cooking.

(c) Vacuum packed joints. These should be thawed in the bag, in the refrigerator or at room temperature. Cook immediately following instructions on packet. Note: If time is short, joints may be thawed in running water, but should be wrapped in a plastic bag to prevent them getting wet.

Cooking Frozen Bacon

All frozen bacon should be cooked immediately it has thawed. The usual cooking methods —boiling, grilling, frying and baking are suitable. Once cooked, the bacon will keep 1–2 days in a refrigerator.

Do not re-freeze after thawing either in the raw or cooked state

Cooked fresh bacon joints should not be frozen as this may result in poor appearance with keeping and flavour problems. Small pieces can be used for flavouring stews or such dishes as Quiche Lorraine which are to be put in the freezer for short periods. The dishes should be well wrapped before freezing.

84

High Quality Storage Life

1. Bacon joints wrapped as recommended:
   - (a) Smoked bacon up to 8 weeks
   - (b) Unsmoked bacon up to 5 weeks
2. Vacuum packed bacon joints up to 10 weeks.
3. Vacuum packed rashers or steaks up to 10 weeks.
4. Foil-wrapped rashers, chops or steaks, smoked, 2–4 weeks only.

Here are a few useful bacon recipes:

Bacon Pasties

12 oz shortcrust pastry
8 oz minced raw steak
6 oz streaky bacon
4 oz lamb's kidney
1 large onion
Salt and pepper
½ teaspoon
   Worcester sauce

Roll out six 7-in. pastry rounds. Chop all ingredients finely and mix well together. Put a spoonful of mixture on each pastry round and form into pasty shapes, sealing edges well. Place on wetted baking sheet and bake at 425°F, 220°C, Gas Mark 7, for 45 minutes. Cool. Pack in foil tray in polythene bag, or in individual polythene bags.

To serve
Thaw 2 hours at room temperature.
High Quality Storage Life   1 month

Hawaiian Gammon Pot Roast

2 lb corner of gammon,
   soaked in cold water
1 pint cider
3 tablespoons white
   vinegar
Dash of Tabasco sauce
Freshly-ground black
   pepper
4 tablespoons honey
8-oz tin pineapple cubes
   and juice
8 oz small peeled
   potatoes
8 oz button mushrooms
2 teaspoons arrowroot,
   2 tablespoons water,
   mixed together

Place the gammon in a pan with cold water. Bring to the boil and simmer for 20–30 minutes. Drain off the liquid. Replace the gammon into a clean pan and pour over the cider, vinegar, Tabasco sauce, pepper, honey, pineapple cubes and juice. Bring to the boil and simmer for 30 minutes. Add the potatoes and cook for a further 15 minutes or until the gammon is tender. Add mushrooms 10 minutes before the end of cooking.
Place the meat in a serving dish and keep hot. Pour a little of the juice on to the arrowroot and water. Return to the pan and bring to the boil, stirring all the time. Pour the sauce over the gammon. Cool and pack for freezing.

To serve
Reheat at 325°F, 170°C, Gas Mark 3, for 1¼ hours.
High Quality Storage Life   2 months

Leftover Bacon

Preparation   Crumble cooked bacon and freeze in small containers.

Serving   Add to casseroles or use on potatoes, cheese or fish dishes. Thaw in refrigerator for 2 hours to use in sandwich spreads.
High Quality Storage Life   2 weeks

FREEZING POULTRY AND GAME

Preparation for Freezing Poultry
Birds to be frozen should be in perfect condition. They should be starved for 24 hours before killing, then hung and bled well. When the bird is plucked, it is important to avoid skin damage; if scalding, beware of over-scalding which may increase the chance of freezer-burn (grey spots occurring during storage). The bird should be cooled in a refrigerator or cold larder for 12 hours, drawn and completely cleaned. With geese and ducks, it is particularly important to see the oil glands are removed as these will cause tainting.

Packing
A whole bird should be carefully trussed to make a neat shape for packing. Birds can be frozen as halves or joints. When packing pieces, it is not always ideal to pack a complete bird in each package; it may be more useful ultimately if all drumsticks are packaged together, all breasts or all wings, according to the way in which the flesh will be cooked.

Giblets have only a storage life of 2 months, so unless a whole bird is to be used within that time, it is not advisable to pack them inside the bird. Giblets should be cleaned, washed, dried and chilled, then wrapped in moisture-vapour-proof paper or a bag, excluding air; frozen in batches, they can be used for soup, stews or pies. Livers should be treated in the same way, and packaged in batches for use in omelettes, risotto or pâté.

Bones of poultry joints should be padded with paper or foil to avoid tearing the freezer wrappings. Joints should be divided by two layers of Cellophane. Bones of young birds may turn brown in storage, but this does not affect flavour or quality.

Stuffings
Stuffing can, if necessary, be put into a bird before freezing, but it is not advisable as the storage life of stuffing is only about 1 month. Pork sausage stuffing should not be used; if a bird must be stuffed, a breadcrumb stuffing is best. It is better to package stuffing separately if some is available when the bird is put into freezer storage; otherwise, it is not worth making specially, as it can easily be prepared while the bird is thawing.

Cooked Poultry
Old birds such as boiling fowls are best frozen after being cooked; the meat should be stripped from the bones, and frozen; or it can be made at once into pies or casseroles, while the carcass is simmered in the cooking liquid to make strong stock for freezing. Slices of

Furred and feathered game are seasonal, but your freezer can make them available at any time of the year.

cooked poultry can be frozen on their own, or in sauce (the latter method is preferable to prevent drying out). If the meat is frozen without sauce, slices should be divided by two sheets of Cellophane and then closely packed together excluding air. Roast and fried poultry frozen to be eaten cold are not particularly successful; on thawing they tend to exude moisture and become flabby.

Thawing

Uncooked poultry must thaw completely before cooking. Thawing in the refrigerator will allow slow, even thawing; thawing at room temperature will be twice as fast but the product will be much less satisfactory. A 4–5 lb. chicken will thaw overnight in a refrigerator and will take 6 hours at room temperature. A turkey weighing 9 lb. will take 36 hours; as much as 3 days should be allowed for a very large bird. A thawed bird can be stored for up to 24 hours in a refrigerator, but no more.

All poultry should be thawed in the unopened freezer wrappings. In an emergency, poultry can be thawed quickly by leaving the bag immersed in running cold water, allowing 30 minutes per lb. thawing time; but this is not advisable in the usual way.

Preparation for Freezing Game

Freeze raw birds or animals which are young and well shot. Roast game is usefully frozen in its season, to eat cold later; but on thawing it exudes moisture so that the flesh may be flabby. Old or badly shot game is usually best converted immediately into made-up dishes such as casseroles.

All game intended for freezing should be hung to its required state *before* freezing, as hanging after thawing will result in the flesh going bad. Grouse, pheasant and partridge should be plucked and drawn before freezing. So should any waterfowl fed on fish. Plover, quail, snipe and woodcock should be plucked but not drawn. Hare and rabbit are handled like poultry. Venison is treated like beef; it is best if aged for 5 to 6 days before freezing if the carcass is in good condition and should be chilled soon after shooting, in a cold larder.

All game should be kept cool between shooting and freezing; care should be taken to remove as much shot as possible, and to make sure the shot wounds are thoroughly clean. Birds should be bled as soon as shot, and then hung to individual taste. After plucking and drawing, the cavity should be thoroughly washed and drained and the body wiped with a damp cloth. The birds should then be packed, cooled and frozen like poultry.

Thawing Game

All game should be thawed in its sealed freezer package; thawing in a refrigerator is more uniform, but of course takes longer. In a refrigerator, allow 5 hours per lb. thawing time; at room temperature, allow 2 hours per lb. Start cooking as soon as game is thawed and still cold, to prevent loss of juices.

88

Here are notes on the preparation, packing, storage and cooking of the various types of poultry and game:

Chicken

Preparation   Hang and cool. Pluck and draw and pack giblets separately. Truss whole bird or cut in joints. Chill 12 hours. Pack in bag, removing air.

Serving   Thaw in bag in refrigerator. Allow 4–5 lb. bird to thaw overnight (6 hours at room temperature).
High Quality Storage Life   12 months

Duck

Preparation   Hang and cool. Remove oil glands. Pluck and draw and pack giblets separately. Chill 12 hours. Pack in bag, removing air.

Serving   Thaw in bag in refrigerator. Allow 4–5 lb. bird to thaw overnight (6 hours at room temperature).
High Quality Storage Life   6 months

Giblets

Preparation   (a) Clean, wash, dry and chill. Pack in bag, removing air. (b) Cook and pack in cooking liquid in box.

Serving   (a) Thaw in bag in refrigerator for 2 hours. (b) Heat gently and use for soups, stews or pies.
High Quality Storage Life   (a) 2 months, (b) 1 month

Goose

Preparation   Hang and cool. Remove oil glands. Pluck and draw and pack giblets separately. Chill 12 hours. Pack in bag, removing air.

Serving   Thaw in bag in refrigerator. Allow small bird to thaw overnight; large bird will need 24 hours.
High Quality Storage Life   6 months

Guinea Fowl

Preparation   Hang and cool. Pluck and draw and pack giblets separately. Truss and chill 12 hours. Pack in bag, removing air.

Serving   Thaw in bag in refrigerator for 8 hours. As this is a dry bird, lard before roasting.
High Quality Storage Life   12 months

Grouse (12th Aug.–10th Dec.) **Partridge** (1st Sept.–1st Feb.)
Pheasant (1st Oct.–1st Feb.)

Preparation   Remove shot and clean wounds. Bleed as soon as shot, keep cool and hang to taste. Pluck, draw and truss. Pad bones. Pack in bag, removing air. If birds are old or badly shot, prepare as casseroles, soups, pies.

Serving   Thaw in bag in refrigerator for 5 hours per lb. (2 hours per lb. at room temperature). Cook as soon as thawed.
High Quality Storage Life   6 months

Hares and Rabbits

Preparation   Clean shot wounds. Behead and bleed as soon as possible, collecting hare's blood if needed for cooking. Hang for 24 hours in a cool place. Skin, clean and wipe. Cut into joints and wrap each piece in cellophane. Pack in usable quantities in bags. Pack blood in box.

Serving   Thaw in bag in refrigerator for 5 hours per lb. (2 hours per lb. at room temperature).
High Quality Storage Life   6 months

Livers

Preparation   Clean, wash, dry and chill. Pack in bag, removing air.

Serving   Thaw in bag in refrigerator for 2 hours.
High Quality Storage Life   2 months

Pigeons

Preparation   Remove shot and clean wounds. Prepare and pack as feathered game. Pigeons are usefully prepared as casseroles or pies for freezing.

Serving   Thaw in bag in refrigerator for 5 hours per lb. (2 hours per lb. at room temperature).
High Quality Storage Life   6 months

Plover, Quail, Snipe, Woodcock

Preparation   Remove shot and clean wounds. Prepare as other feathered game but do not draw. Pad bones. Pack in bag, removing air.

Serving   Thaw in bag in refrigerator for 5 hours per lb. (2 hours per lb. at room temperature). Cook as soon as thawed.
High Quality Storage Life   6 months

Duck roasted when completely thawed and served with traditional vegetables and Cranberry Sauce (p. 61).

Stuffing

Preparation (a) Prepare stuffing to standard recipe. Pack in box or bag. (b) Prepare stuffing and form into balls. Deep-fry, cool and pack into box or bag.

Serving (a) Thaw in bag in refrigerator for 2 hours. (b) Thaw in bag in refrigerator for 2 hours. Put into roasting tin or casserole 10 minutes before serving. *High Quality Storage Life* 1 month

Turkey

Preparation Hang and cool. Pluck and draw, and pack giblets separately. Truss whole or cut in joints. Chill for 12 hours. Pack in bag, removing air.

Serving Thaw in bag in refrigerator for 2 days (small birds); 3 days (large birds). *High Quality Storage Life* 12 months

Venison

Preparation Clean shot wounds. Keep the carcase cold until butchered. Behead, bleed, skin and clean, wash and wipe flesh. Hang in a cool place for 5 days. Joint and pack in bags, removing air. Freeze the good joints, but prepare other cuts as cooked dishes for freezing.

Serving Thaw in wrappings in refrigerator for 4 hours. Remove from wrappings and put into marinade. Continue thawing, allowing 5 hours per lb. Lard meat for roasting. Use the marinade for gravy or casseroles. For the marinade, which will prevent the meat from being dry when cooked, mix $\frac{1}{2}$ pint red wine, $\frac{1}{2}$ pint vinegar, 1 large sliced onion, parsley, thyme and bayleaf. Turn the venison frequently while marinading. *High Quality Storage Life* 8 months

Here are some good freezer recipes for poultry and game:

Farmhouse Chicken

4 *chicken portions*
2 *onions*
Pinch of tarragon
$\frac{3}{4}$ *pint chicken stock*
2–3 *carrots*
1 *green pepper*

Coat the chicken with flour and fry quickly to seal the meat. Transfer to a casserole. Fry the chopped onions, sliced carrots and green pepper in the fat and add these to the chicken. Pour the stock over the vegetables and chicken, season and cook in the oven, with the lid on the casserole, for $1\frac{1}{4}$ hours at 350°F, 180°C, Gas Mark 4. Pack and freeze.

To serve
Reheat at 325°F, 170°C, Gas Mark 3, for 1 hour, stirring in 5 fl. oz. single cream just before serving.
High Quality Storage Life 1 month

Creamed chicken garnished with fresh sliced mushrooms and chopped peppers.

Creamed Chicken

4 chicken pieces
1 pint chicken stock
1 small onion
2 oz button mushrooms
1 tablespoon chopped
* parsley*
1 tablespoon cornflour
Salt and pepper

Brown chicken lightly on all sides in a little butter. Add chopped onion and sliced mushrooms and cook until just soft. Pour on chicken stock (this can be made with a cube if liked) and simmer for 45 minutes. Blend cornflour with a little cold water, and stir into chicken liquid. Add parsley and season lightly. Cool completely. Put chicken pieces into container, pour over sauce, seal and freeze.

To serve
Put into covered oven dish and heat at 350°F, 180 C, Gas Mark 4, for 45 minutes. Serve with rice and peas.
High Quality Storage Life   2 months

Deep Chicken Pie

1 boiling chicken
3 rashers bacon
1 tablespoon chopped
* parsley*
Pinch of mixed herbs
Salt and pepper
12 oz shortcrust pastry

Boil the chicken for about 3 hours until tender. Take flesh from the bones and put in layers in a foil pie-dish, alternating with finely chopped bacon and parsley and a sprinkling of mixed herbs. Season lightly and cover with a gravy made from the chicken stock thickened with a little cornflour. Cool and cover with pastry. Bake at 450°F, 230°C, Gas Mark 8, for 45 minutes. Cool completely. Pack by putting foil dish into polythene bag.

To serve
Reheat at 350°F, 180°C, Gas Mark 4, for 45 minutes. Pie may be frozen with uncooked pastry, and should then be baked straight from freezer at 450°F, 230°C, Gas Mark 8, for 1 hour.
High Quality Storage Life   2 months

Royal Chicken

8 chicken pieces
4 oz bacon
2 oz butter
4 small onions
4 oz mushrooms
½ pint red wine
1 gill stock
Bay leaf, thyme and
    parsley
Salt and pepper
1 tablespoon flour

Wipe the chicken joints. Cut bacon into dice. Melt half the butter and fry the onions until golden, then the bacon and chicken. Add sliced mushrooms, stock, herbs, salt and pepper, cover and cook slowly until the chicken is tender. Take out chicken and mushrooms and keep hot. Skim fat from gravy, and stir in wine. Melt remaining butter, add flour and stir. Add the chicken gravy and simmer until creamy and smooth. Pour over chicken and cool completely. Pack in foil or rigid plastic container, making sure chicken pieces are covered in sauce.

To serve
Put into casserole and heat at 325°F, 170°C, Gas Mark 3, for 1 hour.
High Quality Storage Life   2 months

Coq au Vin

2 × 3 lb chicken
8 oz bacon
20 small white onions
2 oz butter
2 oz oil
2 tablespoons brandy
Salt and pepper
1 tablespoon tomato
    purée
1 pint red wine
Parsley, thyme and
    bayleaf
Pinch of nutmeg
12 oz button mushrooms
1 garlic clove
1 tablespoon cornflour

Chicken joints may be used for this dish; otherwise clean and joint chickens. Cut bacon into small strips, simmer in water for 10 minutes and drain. Peel the onions. Melt the butter and oil and lightly fry bacon until brown. Remove from pan and then brown the onions and remove from pan. Fry chicken joints until golden (about 10 minutes), then add bacon and onions. Cover and cook over low heat for 10 minutes. Add brandy and ignite, rotating the pan until the flame dies out. Add salt and pepper, tomato purée, wine, herbs and nutmeg, and crushed garlic and simmer on stove or in oven for 1 hour. Remove chicken pieces and put into freezer container. Cook mushrooms in a little butter and add to chicken pieces. Thicken gravy with cornflour, cool, and pour over chicken and mushrooms. Pack by covering container with lid or foil.

To serve
Put chicken and sauce in covered dish and heat at 400°F, 200°C, Gas Mark 6, for 45 minutes.
High Quality Storage Life   1 month

Chicken Puffs with Sour Cream Sauce

12 chicken drumsticks
Liver pâté
1 lb puff pastry

Wrap the chicken drumsticks in foil and then roast, boil, poach or grill until tender. Remove the skin and allow to cool. Spread pâté on to chicken drumsticks. Cut out strips of puff pastry and wind round drumsticks from top to bottom. Bake in a hot oven at 425°F, 220°C, Gas Mark 7, until the pastry is cooked, about 25 minutes. Cool and freeze.

To serve
Reheat or serve cold with various sauces based on sour cream, such as: (a) chopped cucumber in sour cream; (b) chopped chives in sour cream.
High Quality Storage Life   1 month

Chicken Maryland

8 frozen chicken
    portions thawed
A little flour
Oil for frying

Place flour and salt in mixing bowl. Make a well in the centre and break in the egg. Add half the milk and beat until smooth. Stir in remaining milk. Dip chicken in flour and shake off any surplus. Roll in coating batter. Fry in shallow fat for 25–30 minutes until tender, turning once. Remove from pan and keep warm.

Coating batter:
4 oz plain flour
¼ level teaspoon salt
1 egg
½ pint milk

Corn fritters, bacon and bananas
4 oz flour
¼ teaspoon salt
1 egg
¼ pint milk
1 teaspoon
    Worcestershire sauce
10 oz thawed frozen
    sweetcorn
1 tablespoon cooking oil
1 oz butter
4 rashers streaky bacon
2 bananas

Place flour and salt in mixing bowl, make a well in the centre and break in the egg. Add half the milk and beat well until smooth. Stir in remaining milk until well blended. Add Worcestershire sauce and sweetcorn. Heat oil and butter in frying pan and drop in tablespoonfuls of sweetcorn batter. Fry until crisp, turning once. Remove from pan and keep warm. Cut bacon rashers in half and make into rolls. Fry until crisp and keep warm. Peel and slice bananas lengthways and fry until lightly browned.

To serve
Arrange chicken portions around edge of dish and place sweetcorn fritters between each portion. Pile bananas in centre and garnish with bacon rolls. Good served with croquette potatoes, asparagus and Brussels sprouts.

95

Turkey Shepherd's Pie

12 oz cooked turkey
1 onion
1 oz butter
Salt and pepper
½ pint milk
8 oz cranberry sauce
2 lb mashed potato
2 oz Cheddar cheese

Mince together the cooked turkey and onion. Melt the butter in a saucepan. Stir in the flour and cook over a low heat for 1 minute. Remove from the heat and gradually stir in the milk. Bring to the boil, stirring all the time to form a smooth sauce. Season to taste. Stir the turkey and onion mixture into the sauce and pour into a 1½-pint freezer tray. Spread the cranberry sauce over the mixture. Pipe or spread the potato over the cranberry sauce and sprinkle with the grated cheese. Cool, cover and freeze.

To serve
Remove the covering and cook at 350°F, 180°C, Gas Mark 4, for 1–1½ hours.
High Quality Storage Life   2 months

Pheasant in Wine

2 young pheasants
12 small onions
2 tablespoons oil
2 tablespoons butter
4 oz small mushrooms
1 pint Burgundy
1 oz plain flour
Salt and pepper

Clean the pheasants. Chop two of the onions with the birds' livers and put half the mixture in each bird. Heat oil and butter together and brown birds all over. Put into a casserole. Remove mushroom stalks and cook in the remaining fat with the wine, until liquid is reduced by half. Mix flour with a little butter and use this to thicken the gravy and pour over the pheasants. Cook onions in boiling salted water until tender, drain and add to casserole. Toss mushrooms in butter and add to other ingredients. Cover and cook at 325°F, 170°C, Gas Mark 3, for 1 hour. Cool. Pack in rigid plastic container or in foil tray.

To serve
Return to casserole and reheat at 325°F, 170°C, Gas Mark 3, for 1 hour. Serve with triangles of fried bread, and garnish with watercress.
High Quality Storage Life   2 months

Normandy Rabbit

1 young rabbit
3 oz butter
4 cloves garlic
1 tablespoon tomato
   purée
½ pint cider
Salt and pepper

Clean and joint the rabbit and simmer for 30 minutes, with a little salt and pepper. Remove meat from bones in large neat pieces, and fry the rabbit with the garlic cloves until golden. Stir in tomato purée, and season with salt and pepper. Simmer for 2 minutes, then pour on cider. Simmer for 5 minutes and cool. Pack in container, covering rabbit pieces with sauce.

To serve
Reheat gently in double boiler and serve garnished with chopped parsley.
High Quality Storage Life   1 month

Hare Soup

1 hare
1 lb lean ham
3 medium onions
Parsley, thyme and
    marjoram
Salt and pepper
3 blades mace
6 pints beef stock
2 rolls
½ pint port

Cut hare into joints and put into a pan with chopped ham and onions, herbs, salt and pepper, mace and stock. Simmer for 2½ hours. Remove meat from bones and put into a blender with the ham, the crumbled rolls and some of the hare liquor which has been strained. Blend until smooth, then mix with remaining hare liquor and port, and simmer for 20 minutes. Cool. Pack in waxed or rigid plastic containers, leaving headspace.

To serve
Reheat gently in double boiler.
High Quality Storage Life   2 months

Duckling Pâté

4 lb duckling
Duck liver
8 oz lean pork
1 garlic clove
Pinch of ground mace
Pinch of grated nutmeg
3 tablespoons dry white
    wine
1 tablespoon dry sherry
Salt and pepper

Roast the duck lightly and then mince the duck meat with the liver and pork twice. Mix this meat with all the other ingredients and pack into a foil container, loaf tin or terrine. Cover with a lid or foil and stand container in a baking tin of water. Cook at 300°F, 150°C, Gas Mark 2, for 1¾ hours, or until the mixture shrinks from the side of the dish. Cool under weights. Pack for freezing.

To serve
Thaw at room temperature for 3 hours.
High Quality Storage Life   2 months

Pigeon Pâté

3 pigeons
⅜th pint (8 fl. oz) red wine
Scant ¼ pint vinegar
1 bay leaf
1 small teaspoon thyme
Grating of nutmeg
Salt and pepper
4 onions
8 oz sausagemeat
1 slice of bread
A little milk

Joint the pigeons. Mix together wine, vinegar, bay leaf, thyme, nutmeg, salt and pepper and finely chopped onions, and pour this over the birds. Leave to soak in cool place for 3 days. Remove flesh from the birds, and mince twice. Mix with sausagemeat. Remove crusts from the bread, and soak in enough milk to moisten the bread. Beat this into the meat mixture. Press mixture into a terrine, loaf tin, or oven dish and cover with a lid or foil. Stand dish in a tin of water, and cook at 350°F, 180°C, Gas Mark 4, for 1½ hours. Cool completely under weights. Remove from baking dish. Pack in heavy-duty foil.

To serve
Thaw at room temperature for 3 hours.
High Quality Storage Life   2 months

Stuffing balls fried before freezing served with thawed roasted chicken.

Poultry Stuffing

for one 3-lb chicken
2 oz suet
4 oz fresh breadcrumbs
2 teaspoons chopped parsley
1 teaspoon chopped thyme
1 teaspoon grated lemon rind
Salt and pepper
1 medium egg

Grate suet and mix all ingredients, binding with beaten egg. *Either* pack into small cartons or polythene bags, but do not stuff birds before freezing. *Or* form mixture into small balls, deep fry, cool, drain and pack in small cartons or polythene bags.

Thawing and serving
Thaw uncooked stuffing in container in refrigerator for 2 hours before stuffing bird. Put cooked stuffing balls into roasting tin with poultry, or into casserole, 10 minutes before serving time.
High Quality Storage Life   1 month

Special Notes
Stuffing containing sausage meat should not be frozen. Basic recipe may have the addition of 2 oz bacon, but then should not be stored for longer than 2 weeks.

Chestnut Stuffing (for turkey)

1 lb chestnuts
2 oz soft white breadcrumbs
1 oz melted butter
2 teaspoons fresh mixed herbs
2 standard eggs
Salt, pepper and dry mustard

Peel chestnuts, and then simmer in a little milk until tender. Sieve and mix with breadcrumbs, butter, herbs and eggs. Add salt and pepper and a pinch of dry mustard. Pack in cartons or polythene bags.
High Quality Storage Life   1 month

FREEZING FISH AND SHELLFISH

Only really fresh fish can be frozen, since it must be processed within 24 hours. Therefore it is not advisable to freeze shop-purchased fish.

Cooked fish can be frozen in sauces or pies, or ready-fried, but it is rarely worth the trouble to cook fish specially for freezing. Fish should never be overcooked and the time taken to reheat will not only spoil flavour and rob the fish of any nutritive value, but will also take as long as the original cooking.

Fatty fish (i.e. haddock, halibut, herring, mackerel, salmon, trout, turbot) will keep for 4 months at most. White fish (i.e. cod, plaice, sole, whiting) will keep for 6 months. Shellfish are best stored no longer than 1 month. It is wise to keep fish for only the shortest possible time in the freezer.

It is interesting to freeze smoked fish such as bloaters, kippers and haddock.

Preparation for Freezing

Since the fish must be fresh, one must clean home-caught fish ready for freezing as soon as it is caught. The fish should be killed at once, scaled if necessary and fins removed. Small fish can be left whole; large fish should have heads and tails removed, or can be divided into steaks. Flat fish and herrings are best gutted, and flat fish skinned and filleted. White fish should be washed well in salted water during cleaning to remove blood and membranes, but fatty fish should be washed in fresh water.

Freezing Methods

There are four ways of preparing fish for freezing, the first two being the most common.

(a) Dry Pack. Separate pieces of fish with double thickness of Cellophane, wrap in moisture-vapour-proof paper, carton or bag, seal and freeze. Be sure the paper is in close contact with the fish to exclude air which will dry the fish and make it tasteless. Freeze quickly on the floor of the freezer.

(b) Brine Pack. (This is *not* suitable for fatty fish, as salt tends to oxidise and lead to rancidity.) Dip fish into cold salted water (1 tablespoon salt to 1 quart water), drain, wrap and seal. Do not keep brine-dipped fish longer than 3 months.

(c) Acid Pack. Citric acid preserves the colour and flavour of fish; ascorbic acid is an anti-oxidant which stops the development of rancidity in fish which can cause off-flavours and smells. A chemist can provide an ascorbic-citric acid powder, to be diluted in a proportion of 1 part powder to 100 parts of water. Dip fish into this solution, drain, wrap and seal.

Frozen mackerel grilled after thawing (see p. 103).

Wrap fish in foil before freezing – and after thawing and grilling.

(d) Solid Ice Pack. Small fish, steaks or fillets can be covered with water in refrigerator trays or loaf tins and frozen into solid blocks. The fish should be separated by double paper as usual. Remove ice blocks from pan, wrap in freezer paper and store. The fish can also be frozen in a solid ice pack in large waxed tubs; cover the fish completely to within $\frac{1}{2}$ in. of container top and crumple a piece of Cellophane over the top of the fish before closing the lid. The only advantage in this solid ice method is a saving of containers and wrapping material.

Freezing Large Whole Fish
Sometimes a large whole fish may be wanted; if so, it can be frozen whole, but is best protected by 'glazing'. Salmon and salmon trout are obvious examples, or perhaps a haddock or halibut to serve stuffed for a party.

To Glaze a Large Fish
First clean the fish. Then place the unwrapped fish against the freezer wall in the coldest possible part of the freezer. When the fish is frozen solid, dip it very quickly into very cold water so a thin coating of ice will form. Return fish to freezer for an hour, and repeat process. Continue until ice has built up to $\frac{1}{4}$ in thickness. The fish can be stored without wrappings for 2 weeks, but is better wrapped in freezer paper for longer storage.

Smoked Fish
Bloaters, kippers and haddock can be wrapped and frozen and will keep for 2 months. No special preparation is necessary.

Freezer-stored raw fish, fresh and smoked, and a starter course using a smoked fish pâté.

Shellfish
Freshly caught shellfish can be frozen immediately after cooking. Scallops and oysters are frozen raw. Shrimps can be frozen when cooked, or after being potted in butter.

Thawing and Cooking
All fish should be thawed slowly in unopened wrappings. A 1-lb. or 1-pint package takes about 3 hours at room temperature, or 6 hours in a refrigerator. Frozen fish may be used for boiling, steaming, grilling or frying; except for frying, complete thawing is not necessary.

Here are notes on preparing, freezing, storing and cooking fish:

Crab

Preparation   Cook, drain and cool. Clean crab and remove edible meat. Pack into boxes or bags.

Serving   Thaw in container in refrigerator. Serve cold, or add to hot dishes.
High Quality Storage Life   1 month

Fatty Fish (Haddock, Halibut, Mackerel, Salmon, Trout, Turbot)

Preparation   Clean. Fillet or cut in steaks if liked, or leave whole. Separate pieces of fish with double thickness of cellophane. Wrap in freezer paper, or put in box or bag. Be sure air is excluded, or fish will be dry and tasteless. Keep pack shallow. Freeze quickly. Large fish may be prepared in solid ice pack. Do not use brine pack:

Serving   Thaw large fish in unopened container in refrigerator. Cook small pieces of fish while frozen.
High Quality Storage Life   1 month

Lobster and Crayfish

Preparation   Cook, cool and split. Remove flesh and pack into boxes or bags.

Serving   Thaw in container in refrigerator. Serve cold, or add to hot dishes.
High Quality Storage Life   1 month

Mussels

Preparation   Scrub very thoroughly and remove any fibrous matter sticking out from the shell. Put in a large saucepan and cover with a damp cloth. Put over medium heat about 3 minutes until they open. Cool in the pan. Remove from shells and pack in boxes, covering with their own juice.

Serving   Thaw in container in refrigerator and cook, using as fresh fish.
High Quality Storage Life   1 month

Oysters

Preparation   Open oysters and save liquid. Wash fish in salt water (1 teaspoon salt to 1 pint water). Pack in boxes, covering with own liquid.

Serving   Thaw in container in refrigerator. Serve raw or cooked.
High Quality Storage Life   1 month

Prawns

Preparation   Cook and cool in cooking water. Remove shells. Pack tightly in boxes or bags.

Serving   Thaw in container in refrigerator. Serve cold, or use for cooking.
High Quality Storage Life   1 month

Foil-wrapped salmon steaks can be cooked in the same foil. Here are raw and cooked steaks from the same catch.

Scallops

Preparation   Open shells. Wash fish in salt water (1 teaspoon salt to 1 pint water). Pack in boxes covering with salt water, and leaving $\frac{1}{2}$ in. headspace.

Serving   Thaw in container in refrigerator. Drain and cook, using as fresh fish.
High Quality Storage Life   1 month

Shrimps

Preparation (a) Cook and cool in cooking water. Remove shells. Pack in boxes or bags. (b) Cook and shell shrimps. Pack in waxed boxes and cover with melted spiced butter.

Serving (a) Thaw in container in refrigerator to eat cold. Add frozen shrimps to hot dishes. (b) Thaw in container in refrigerator.
High Quality Storage Life 1 month

Smoked Fish (Bloaters, Eel, Haddock, Kippers, Mackerel, Salmon, Sprats, Trout)

Preparation Pack fish in layers with Cellophane between. Keep pack shallow.

Serving To eat cold, thaw in refrigerator. Haddock and kippers may be cooked while frozen.
High Quality Storage Life 2 months

White Fish (Cod, Plaice, Sole, Whiting)

Preparation Clean. Fillet or cut in steaks if liked, or leave whole. Separate pieces of fish with double thickness of Cellophane. Wrap in freezer paper, or put in box or bag. Be sure air is excluded, or fish will be dry and tasteless. Keep pack shallow. Freeze quickly.

Serving Thaw large fish in unopened container in refrigerator. Cook small pieces of fish while frozen.
High Quality Storage Life 3 months

The following recipes are good for freezing, or use frozen fish:

Fish Pie (Pastry)

½ lb cooked haddock or
   cod (fresh or smoked)
3 tomatoes
4 oz button mushrooms
Juice of ½ lemon
1 tablespoon chopped
   parsley
1 oz butter
1 oz flour
½ pint milk
Salt and pepper
Pinch of ground mace
½ lb flaky or puff pastry
Beaten egg to glaze

Cut the cooked fish into even-sized pieces, and arrange in layers with the tomatoes and mushrooms in the bottom of a pie dish. Sprinkle with parsley and lemon juice. Melt the butter in a saucepan and stir in the flour. Gradually blend in the milk, and stir over a gentle heat until the sauce thickens. Season with salt and pepper and a pinch of mace. Pour over the fish. Cool and freeze.

To serve
Roll out the pastry to a little larger than the pie dish. Cut off a thin strip of pastry and press round the rim of the dish using a little water to seal. Brush with water. Lift the remaining pastry and cover pie dish. Press edges together to seal, cut away surplus with a knife and decorate as required. Brush with beaten egg and place in oven at 400°F, 200°C, Gas Mark 6, and cook for 45 minutes or until the pastry is cooked and the filling thawed.
High Quality Storage Life 1 month

Coley Jalousie

*1 small pkt frozen
  puff pastry*
$\frac{1}{2}$ oz margarine or butter
$\frac{3}{8}$ oz flour
$\frac{1}{4}$ pint milk
$\frac{1}{2}$ oz tomato purée
$\frac{1}{2}$ teaspoon salt
1 small onion
*$\frac{1}{2}$ lb coley (cooked and
  flaked)*
Egg to glaze
*Garnish with quartered
  tomatoes and prawns*

Melt butter or margarine and stir in flour, cook the roux for a few moments. Remove the saucepan from heat and stir in milk, return to heat and bring back to the boil, stirring continuously. Season the sauce, and add the cooked flaked fish, very finely chopped onion and tomato puree. Cover this mixture and put aside to cool.

Divide the pastry in half, roll out the first half to form a rectangle. Place on a baking sheet and spread with cool fish mixture, leaving a $\frac{1}{2}$-in. border around the edge of the pastry. Roll out the second half of the pastry the same size as the first. Fold this piece of pastry in half length-ways, and make a series of diagonal cuts down the folded edge to within about a $\frac{1}{2}$ in. of the cut edge, to form a herringbone pattern when unfolded.

Brush lightly with water around the edge, and fit over the fish mixture, seal the edges to the bottom layer of the pastry. Knock up the edges with a knife, and glaze with beaten egg. Cook at 425°F, 220°C, Gas Mark 6, for about 30 minutes, until golden brown. Cool, wrap and freeze.

To serve
Reheat at 350°F, 180°C, Gas Mark 4, for 45 minutes and serve hot with peas or a salad.
High Quality Storage Life   1 month

If you freeze scallops keep the shells for dishes like these Scallops with Dutch Sauce.

Scallops with Dutch Sauce

4 medium-sized scallops
$\frac{1}{8}$th pint milk
1 oz butter
1 oz cornflour
Mashed potato for piped borders
4 oz grated Gouda cheese
Salt and pepper to taste

Prepare the scallops, keeping only the white and orange parts, and the deep shells (and liquor if you get it). Rinse if fresh. Poach in a little milk or milk and scallop liquor until tender, between 7 and 10 minutes. Brush the shells with melted butter. Pipe a border of mashed potato round the edge of each shell, and place the scallops in the shells.

Use a frozen basic sauce or make a cheese sauce with the butter, cornflour and almost all the grated cheese. Pour the sauce over the scallops. Sprinkle with the remaining cheese and a few breadcrumbs. Place under a hot grill for 5 minutes.

To serve
Thaw 2 hours at room temperature. Reheat 7–10 minutes in a low oven.
High Quality Storage Life 1 month

Plaice Goujons with Tartare Sauce

8 frozen plaice fillets
    thawed and skinned
1½ oz seasoned flour
Oil for frying

Sauce:
½ pint mayonnaise
1 tablespoon lemon juice
2 teaspoons washed,
    chopped capers
2 teaspoons washed,
    chopped gherkins
2 teaspoons chopped
    parsley
Lemon slices to garnish

Cut plaice fillets diagonally across the grain, into strips about ½-in. wide. Coat in seasoned flour and fry in deep fat, heated to 180° C (350° F) Gas Mark 4 for 2–3 minutes until crisp and golden-brown. Drain and keep warm.

For tartare sauce: mix together all ingredients and place in a small bowl.

Place goujons on a plate surrounding the sauce and garnish with lemon twists.

Seaflan

6 oz short crust pastry
2 frozen cod steaks
4 oz thawed frozen
    prawns
2 eggs
¼ pint milk
2 tablespoons chopped
    parsley
2 teaspoons lemon juice
Salt and pepper

Roll out pastry and use to line an 8-in. flan ring. Bake 'blind' at 200° C (400° F) Gas Mark 6 for 15 minutes. Cook cod according to pack instructions and flake coarsely. Reserve a few prawns for garnish and place remainder in base of partially cooked flan case with the flaked cod. Beat eggs and milk together, add parsley and lemon juice and season to taste. Pour over fish and bake at 180° C (350° F) Gas Mark 4 for about 30 minutes until set and golden-brown. Garnish with reserved prawns. Cool, pack in foil, seal, label and freeze.

To serve
Reheat at 180° C (350° F) Gas Mark 4 for 30 minutes. Serve warm.
High Quality Storage Life   1 month

Kipper Pizza Wheel

Scone dough:
8 oz self-raising flour
½ level teaspoon salt
2 oz butter or
    margarine
¼ pint milk

Topping:
1 oz butter
8 oz sliced onions
8 oz tomatoes
4 oz grated cheese
1 7-oz packet frozen
    kipper fillets, thawed
Parsley sprig to garnish

For scone dough: rub fat into flour and salt until mixture resembles fine breadcrumbs. Stir in milk to give a soft dough. Knead lightly on a floured surface and roll out to an 8-in. circle and place on a greased baking tray.
For topping: melt butter in pan and fry onions for 5 minutes until soft. Spread on top of scone dough. Slice tomatoes and arrange on top and cover with grated cheese. Cut kipper fillets into ½-in. strips and arrange on top radiating from the centre.

Bake pizza at 220° C (425° F) Gas Mark 7 for about 20 minutes until golden. Cool and wrap in foil. Seal, label and freeze.

To serve
Wrap lightly in foil and reheat at 180° C (350° F) Gas Mark 4, for about 30 minutes. Serve warm, garnished with parsley.
High Quality Storage Life   1 month

Seaflan, Plaice Goujons with Tartare Sauce and Kipper Pizza Wheel are all made simply from commercially frozen fish. Used with other commercial products they can form the basis for a teenage party.

Fishfinger and Bacon Sticks

6 frozen fish fingers
4 oz streaky bacon
1 oz butter or oil
Cocktail sticks

Cut fish fingers into 3 cubes. Remove rind from bacon, cut each rasher into 3 and roll up. Place fish finger cubes and bacon rolls under grill, brush with melted butter or oil and cook for about 5 minutes turning once until cooked. Place a fish finger cube and bacon roll on each cocktail stick. Serve on a plate or stick into a melon.

Kedgeree

4 oz long grain rice
8 oz cooked smoked
  haddock fillet (12 oz
  raw)
2 oz unsalted butter
2 teaspoons lemon juice
Pepper and salt to taste
1 tablespoon chopped
  fresh parsley

Cook the rice in plenty of fast boiling salted water until *just* tender. Drain and spread out to dry and cool. Free the haddock of all skin and bone, and flake the fish coarsely. When both are quite cold mix the rice and haddock together thoroughly, and add other ingredients. Fill into a suitable container, seal, label and freeze.

NOTE
Use a firm rice which retains its texture, and take care to under rather than overcook it in the first instance. Italian long grain rice gives very good results. Cook the rice in plain salted water, not in the liquid in which the fish was cooked, and use unsalted butter. Hard-boiled egg toughens ·on freezing, so use a freshly cooked egg for garnishing at serving time. You can also garnish with thawed frozen prawns.

To serve
Heat gently, breaking up the frozen block with a fork. Cover, and cook over *low* heat, stirring now and then until hot through. Pile up on a hot serving dish and garnish with sliced freshly-cooked, hard-boiled egg.
High Quality Storage Life　1 month

Fish Cakes

1 lb cooked white fish
1 lb mashed potato
4 teaspoons chopped
  parsley
2 oz butter
Salt and pepper
2 small eggs

Mix flaked fish, potato, parsley, melted butter and seasonings together and bind with egg. Divide the mixture into sixteen pieces and form into flat rounds. Coat with egg and breadcrumbs and fry until golden. Cool quickly. Pack in polythene bags or foil containers, separating fish cakes with waxed paper or Cellophane. Fish cakes may also be frozen uncovered on baking sheets and packed when solid.

To serve
Reheat in oven or frying-pan with a little fat, allowing 5 minutes' cooking on each side.
High Quality Storage Life　1 month

Potted Shrimps

Shrimps
Butter
Salt and pepper
Ground mace and cloves
  to taste

Cook freshly caught shrimps, cool in cooking liquid and shell. Pack tightly into waxed cartons. Melt butter, season with salt, pepper and a little mace and cloves. Cool butter and pour over shrimps. Chill until cold. Pack by covering with lids and sealing with freezer tape.

To serve
Thaw in containers at room temperature for 2 hours, or heat in double boiler until butter has melted and shrimps are warm to serve on toast.
High Quality Storage Life   3 months

Cod's Roe Pâté

24 oz smoked cod's roe
½ pint double cream
2 crushed garlic cloves
Juice of 1 lemon
2 dessertspoons olive oil
Black pepper
Cucumber and mint
  sprigs to garnish

Scrape roe into bowl and mix to a smooth paste with cream, garlic, lemon, oil and pepper. Pack into small containers with lids.

To serve
Thaw in refrigerator for 3 hours, stirring occasionally to blend ingredients. Serve in stemmed glasses or glass bowls, decorated with cucumber and mint springs.
High Quality Storage Life   1 month

Seafood Mousse

½-pint packet aspic
  powder
8 oz cooked lobster, crab
  or scampi
1 tablespoon dry white
  wine
¼ pint double cream
Salt and Cayenne
  pepper

Make up the aspic as directed on the packet, but with only ¼ pint water. Leave until cold. Pound together the shellfish and wine, and put the mixture through a sieve (or whirl it in a blender). Gradually add the aspic, a little at a time. Whip the cream to a soft peak and gradually fold into the crab mixture. It is best if this is done with the crab mixture in a bowl on crushed ice. Add salt and Cayenne pepper to taste. Put into a soufflé dish, cover and freeze.

To serve
Thaw in refrigerator for 3 hours and garnish with chopped parsley.
High Quality Storage Life   2 months

Crab and Cheese Dip

2 oz Danish Blue cheese
2 oz cream cheese
½ teaspoon Worcester
  sauce
1 clove garlic
1 teaspoon lemon juice
6 oz fresh or canned
  crabmeat

Blend together cheeses and gradually work in sauce, crushed garlic, lemon juice and crabmeat. Pack in waxed or rigid plastic container.

To serve
Thaw in refrigerator for 3 hours and serve in a bowl surrounded by crisps.
High Quality Storage Life   2 weeks

FREEZING DAIRY PRODUCE

Dairy produce should not be allowed to take up much freezer space. But it can be useful to freeze quantities of cheap fat or eggs when available; cheese left after large parties; leftover egg yolks or whites or cracked eggs bought cheaply, or thick cream brought back from a country holiday.

Butter or Margarine

Preparation   Overwrap blocks in foil or polythene.

Serving   Thaw enough for one week's use.
High Quality Storage Life   6 months (unsalted); 3 months (salted)

Cheese

Preparation   (a) Freeze hard cheese such as Cheddar in small portions (8 oz or less). Divide slices with double Cellophane and wrap in foil or freezer paper.
(b) Freeze grated cheese in polythene bags; the pieces remain separated.
(c) Freeze Camembert, Port Salut, Stilton, Danish Blue and Roquefort with careful sealing to avoid drying out and cross-contamination.

Serving   (a) Thaw in open wrappings at room temperature for 2 hours. Cut while slightly frozen to avoid crumbling. (b) Sprinkle on dishes or thaw for 1 hour before adding to sauces. (c) Thaw 1 day in refrigerator and 1 day at room temperature for full flavour.
High Quality Storage Life   (a) 3 months, (b) 3 months, (c) 6 months

Frozen grated cheese is useful for flavouring sauces or for making cheese flans.

Cottage Cheese

Preparation   Freeze in waxed tubs or rigid plastic containers. Freeze quickly to avoid water separation.

Serving   Thaw in container in refrigerator overnight.
High Quality Storage Life   3 months

Cream

Preparation   Use pasteurised cream, over 40% butterfat. Freeze in cartons (1 in. headspace).

Serving   Thaw in container at room temperature. Beat lightly with a fork to make smooth. Note that in hot drinks, oil will rise to the surface.
High Quality Storage Life   6 months

Cream Cheese

Preparation   Best blended with heavy cream and frozen as a cocktail dip in waxed tubs or rigid plastic containers.

Serving   Thaw in container in refrigerator overnight. Blend with a fork to make smooth.
High Quality Storage Life   3 months

Eggs

Preparation   Do not freeze eggs in shell. Blend lightly with a fork. Add $\frac{1}{2}$ teaspoon salt or $\frac{1}{2}$ teaspoon sugar to 5 eggs. Pack in waxed or rigid plastic containers. Label with number of eggs and 'salt' or 'sugar'.

Serving   Thaw in unopened container in refrigerator. Use as fresh eggs as soon as thawed. 3 tablespoons whole egg = 1 fresh egg.
High Quality Storage Life   12 months

Egg Whites

Preparation   Freeze in waxed or rigid plastic containers or in ice-cube trays. Label with number of whites.

Serving   Thaw in refrigerator, but bring to room temperature before use. Can be whipped successfully.
High Quality Storage Life   12 months

Egg Yolks

Preparation   Mix lightly with a fork. Add $\frac{1}{2}$ teaspoon salt or $\frac{1}{2}$ tablespoon sugar to 6 yolks. Label with number of yolks and 'salt' or 'sugar'. Can be frozen in waxed or rigid plastic containers or in ice-cube trays. Transfer cubes to polythene bags for storage.

Serving   Thaw in refrigerator. Use alone or mix with whites.
High Quality Storage Life   12 months

Milk

Preparation   Freeze homogenised milk in cartons (1 in. headspace).

Serving   Thaw at room temperature and use quickly.
High Quality Storage Life   1 month

Whipped Cream

Preparation   Use 1 tablespoon sugar to 1 pint cream. (a) Freeze in cartons (1 in. head-space). (b) Pipe in rosettes, freeze on open trays and pack in boxes.

Serving   Thaw in container at room temperature. Rosettes will thaw in 15 minutes at room temperature.
High Quality Storage Life   6 months

Orange Cheese Dip

4 oz full fat soft cheese
1 tablespoon grated orange rind
$\frac{1}{4}$ teaspoon salt
Pinch of paprika

Blend together cheese, orange rind, salt and paprika. Pack in waxed or rigid plastic container.

To serve
Thaw in refrigerator for 3 hours, and serve in a bowl with crisps.
High Quality Storage Life   2 weeks

Quiche Lorraine

4 oz shortcrust pastry
$\frac{1}{2}$ oz butter
1 small onion
1 oz streaky bacon
1 egg and 1 egg yolk
2 oz grated cheese
1 gill creamy milk
Pepper

Line a flan ring with pastry, or line a foil dish which can be put into the freezer. Gently soften chopped onion and bacon in butter until golden, and put into pastry case. Lightly beat together egg, egg yolk, cheese, milk and pepper. Add a little salt if the bacon is not very salty. Pour into flan case. Bake at 375°F, 190°C, Gas Mark 5, for 30 minutes. Cool. Pack in foil in rigid container to avoid breakage, and seal with freezer tape.

To serve
Thaw in refrigerator for 6 hours to serve cold. If preferred hot, heat at 350°F, 180°C, Gas Mark 4, for 20 minutes.
High Quality Storage Life   2 months

Macaroni Cheese

8 oz macaroni
4 oz butter
4 tablespoons flour
1½ pints milk
10 oz cheese
1 teaspoon salt
Pepper

Optional – chopped ham, chopped cooked onions or mushrooms. Cook macaroni as directed and drain well. Melt butter, blend in flour and work in milk, cooking to a smooth sauce. Over low heat, stir in cheese and seasoning. Mix macaroni and cheese and cool. Pack into foil container.

To serve
Cover with foil and heat at 400°F, 200°C, Gas Mark 6, for 1 hour, removing foil for the last 15 minutes to brown top.
High Quality Storage Life 2 months

ICE CREAM

Home-made ice cream can be stored in the freezer for 3 months. Bought ice cream is best stored no longer than 1 month. If large containers of bought ice cream are stored, and not repackaged into serving sizes before storage, they should be used sooner than this after opening. When portions have been taken out of a large container, a piece of foil over the unused portion will help to retain flavour and texture.

Home-made ice cream for the freezer is best made with pure cream and gelatine or egg yolks. For immediate use, evaporated milk may be used, but the flavour is less good (before using the unopened tin of milk should be boiled for 10 minutes, cooled and left in a

Ice cream sundaes with fruits from your freezer make delicious desserts in a moment.

refrigerator overnight). A smooth commercial product cannot be produced from a home freezer. The ingredients are different and so is the equipment which gives a smooth ice cream. Crank attachments can now be bought for freezers, however, which work on the principle of the old dasher–churn, giving a constant beating which produces a relatively smooth product.

All home-made ice cream should be frozen quickly, or it will be 'grainy'. The correct emulsifying agent will help to make a smooth product. Egg, gelatine, cream or sugar syrup will stop large ice crystals forming; gelatine gives a particularly smooth ice. Whipped egg whites give lightness. Freezing diminishes sweetness, but too much sugar will prevent freezing. The correct proportion is one part sugar to four parts liquid.

Preparation for Freezing Ice Cream

Whatever emulsifying agent is used, the preparation is similar. The mixture should be packed into trays and frozen until just solid about ½ in. from the edge. The mixture should then be beaten quickly in a chilled bowl, and then frozen again for a further hour. This 'freezing and beating' technique should be repeated for up to three hours. Some freezer owners save time by packing the ice cream into storage containers and freezing after the first beating, but results are less smooth, and it is preferable to complete the ice cream before packing for storage. To remove portions of ice cream from a large container, dip a scoop into boiling water before cutting into the ice cream.

To make moulds of ice cream, press the finished ice into metal moulds (if double-sided moulds are not available, use metal jelly moulds, cover tops with foil, wrap and seal). To turn out, invert mould on plate and cover metal with cloth wrung out in hot water. Two-flavoured moulds can be made by lining mould with one flavour and filling with another (chopped fruit or nuts may be added to the inner ice cream).

Basic Ice Cream

Preparation Prepare standard recipe and freeze in trays. When completed, pack in rigid plastic boxes, filling air space with crumpled foil or Cellophane. Seal tightly.

Serving Scoop out into dishes. Fill remaining airspace in container with crumpled foil or Cellophane.
High Quality Storage Life 3 months

Fresh Fruit Ices

Preparation Prepare standard recipe and freeze in trays. Add pieces of fresh fruit before final freezing. Pack in rigid plastic boxes, filling air space with crumpled foil or Cellophane. Seal tightly.

Serving Scoop out into dishes. Fill remaining air space in container with crumpled foil or Cellophane.
High Quality Storage Life 3 months

Moulds or Bombes

Preparation Use double-sided moulds, jelly moulds or pudding basins. Soften ice cream slightly and line the mould. Freeze for 1 hour, then put in the next layer of ice cream. Freeze again then add another ice cream, or a filling of fruit and/or liqueur. Wrap in foil, seal and freeze.

Serving Turn out on chilled plate, using cloth wrung out in hot water. Wrap in foil and freeze 1 hour before serving.
High Quality Storage Life 3 months

Sorbets

Preparation (a) Pack in leakproof rigid plastic or waxed containers and seal tightly, as these water ices do not freeze completely hard during storage. (b) Pack into clean orange or lemon skins and wrap in foil, sealing tightly.

Serving (a) Scoop on to plates or fill fresh fruit skins. (b) Remove foil and return to freezer for 1 hour to frost the skins.
High Quality Storage Life 3 months

Custard Ice

¾ *pint creamy milk*
1 vanilla pod
2 large egg yolks
2 oz sugar
Small pinch of salt
⅓ *pint thick cream*

Scald milk with vanilla pod. Remove pod and pour milk on to egg yolks lightly beaten with sugar and salt. Cook mixture in a double boiler until it coats the back of a spoon. Cool and strain and stir in the cream. Pour into freezing trays and beat twice during a total freezing time of about 3 hours. Pack into containers, cover and seal, and store in freezer.

Gelatine Ice

¾ *pint creamy milk*
1 vanilla pod
1 dessertspoon gelatine
3 oz sugar
Pinch of salt

Heat ¼-pint milk with vanilla pod to boiling point. Soak gelatine in 2 tablespoons cold water, then put into a bowl standing in hot water until the gelatine is syrupy. Pour warm milk on to the gelatine, stir in sugar, salt and remaining milk. Remove vanilla pod and freeze mixture, beating twice during 3 hours total freezing time. Pack into containers, cover and seal, and store in freezer. This mixture is particularly good for using with such flavourings such as chocolate or caramel.

Cream Ice

1 pint single cream
1 vanilla pod
3 oz sugar
Pinch of salt

Scald cream with vanilla pod, stir in sugar and salt, and cool. Remove vanilla pod and freeze mixture to a mush. Beat well in a chilled bowl and continue freezing (about 2 hours total freezing time). Pack into containers, cover, seal and label, and store in freezer.

Flavouring for Ice Creams, Basic

Flavourings should be strong and pure (e.g. vanilla pod or sugar instead of essence; liqueurs rather than flavoured essences), as they are affected by low temperature storage. Flavourings may be varied by using one of the basic recipes and adjusting to the required flavour.
Butterscotch Cook the sugar in the recipe with 2 tablespoons butter until well browned, then add to hot milk or cream.
Caramel Melt half the sugar in the recipe with a moderate heat, using a heavy saucepan, and add slowly to the hot milk.
Chocolate Melt 2 oz unsweetened cooking chocolate in 4 tablespoons hot water, stir until smooth, and add to the hot milk.
Coffee Scald 2 tablespoons ground coffee with milk or cream and strain before adding to other ingredients.

Ice creams stored in foil pudding basins can be scooped, or unmoulded and served with sauce.

Peppermint Use oil of peppermint, and colour lightly green.
Praline Make as caramel flavouring, adding 4 oz blanched, toasted and finely chopped almonds.
Egg Nog Stir in several tablespoons rum, brandy or whisky to ice cream made with egg yolks.
Ginger Add 2 tablespoons chopped preserved ginger and 3 tablespoons ginger syrup to basic mixture.
Maple Use maple syrup in place of sugar, add 4 oz chopped walnuts.
Pistachio Add 1 teaspoon almond essence and 2 oz chopped pistachio nuts, and colour lightly green.

Flavourings for Ice Creams, Mixed

Mixed flavour ice creams can be prepared by adding flavoured sauces or crushed fruit to vanilla ice cream, or by making additions to some of the basic flavours. Crushed fruit such as strawberries, raspberries or canned mandarin oranges may be beaten into vanilla ice cream before packing. Chocolate or butterscotch sauce can be swirled through vanilla ice. Chopped toasted nuts or crushed nut toffee pair with vanilla, coffee or chocolate flavours. A pinch of coffee powder may be used in chocolate ice cream, or a little melted chocolate in coffee ice; one of the chocolate- or coffee-flavoured liqueurs may also be used.

Coffee Ice

4 heaped tablespoons freshly-ground coffee
1 pint water
3 oz caster sugar
½ pint single cream

Put coffee into a hot dry coffee pot, pour on boiling water, and leave to stand for 10 minutes. Strain and mix with sugar. Cool and mix with cream. Freeze for 45 minutes, stir and continue freezing for 1½ hours. Pack in waxed or rigid plastic containers.

To serve
Pile into small cups and serve with sweet biscuits.
High Quality Storage Life 2 months

120

Ice-Cream Layer Cake with strawberries.

Brown Bread Ice Cream

$\frac{1}{2}$ *pint double cream*
$\frac{1}{4}$ *pint single cream*
3 oz sieved icing sugar
4 oz brown breadcrumbs
  from a day-old loaf
1 tablespoon rum
2 eggs, separated

Whisk double cream until just stiff and gradually whisk in single cream. Fold in icing sugar and breadcrumbs. Mix together rum and egg yolks and fold in. Whisk egg whites until almost stiff and fold into mixture. Pour into freezing trays or 2 pint polythene container and freeze until firm. This ice cream does not need beating during freezing.

To serve
Scoop into small glasses and serve with sweet biscuits and fresh fruit.

Ice-Cream Layer Cake

$\frac{1}{2}$ *gallon strawberry ice*
  cream
$\frac{1}{2}$ *gallon vanilla ice*
  cream
16 tablespoons
  strawberry jam
1 lb strawberries
2 pints double cream

Slightly soften ice creams and press into sponge cake tins to make 4 strawberry layers and 4 vanilla layers. Cover each tin with foil and freeze until firm. Unmould ice cream and arrange in 2 stacks of alternate layers spread with strawberry jam (this is best done on a foil-covered cake board). Cover with whipped cream and strawberries and freeze uncovered for three hours. Wrap in foil for storage.
Note: This cake may be made without the cream and strawberries, which can be added just before serving. Fresh strawberries may also be chopped and added to the strawberry ice cream before moulding in the tins.

FREEZING BREAD, CAKES, PASTRY AND SANDWICHES

Preparation for Freezing Bread and Cakes

Small cakes, buns and rolls are most easily frozen in polythene bags; small iced cakes are better packed in boxes. Large quantities of small iced cakes can be frozen in single layers, then packed in larger boxes with Cellophane or greaseproof paper between the layers. Bread and large cakes can both be frozen in polythene bags. While it is usually most convenient to pack cakes whole, some families may need meal-size wedges or individual pieces for lunch-boxes. These pieces can be frozen individually in bags or boxes, but it is easier to slice the whole cake in wedges before freezing, and take slices as needed without thawing the whole cake.

When making cakes for freezing, it is most important to use good ingredients. Stale flour deteriorates quickly after freezing, so it is important to use fresh flour. Butter cakes retain a good flavour, but margarine is more suitable for strongly-flavoured cakes such as chocolate, and it always gives a good light texture. Eggs should be fresh and very well beaten, as whites and yolks freeze at different speeds and this can affect the texture of the cake. Icings for freezing are best made with butter and icing sugar; cakes should *not* be filled with boiled icing or with cream as these will crumble on thawing; so will icings made with egg whites. Fruit fillings and jams will make a cake soggy, and are best added after thawing. Flavourings must always be pure, as synthetics develop off-flavours in storage (this is particularly important with vanilla, and only pure extract or vanilla sugar made with a pod should be used). If the freezer user is not an enthusiastic bread or cake cook, there is no reason why bought cakes should not be frozen for emergencies. Buns, Dundee cakes, unfilled sponges and sponge flan cases all freeze well and are very useful, but the same limitations concerning icings and fillings will apply to bought cakes as to home-baked ones. Crumpets and muffins are bought seasonal delicacies which can be frozen for future use.

Uncooked Yeast Mixtures

It is possible to freeze unbaked bread and buns for up to 2 weeks, but proving after freezing takes a long time, and the final texture may be heavier. If unbaked dough is frozen, it should be allowed to prove once, and either shaped for baking or kept in bulk if storage in this form is easier. Brush the surface with a little olive oil or unsalted melted butter to prevent toughening of the crust, and add a little extra sugar to sweet mixtures.

Single loaves or a quantity of dough can be packed in freezer paper or polythene, and rolls can be packed in layers separated by Cellophane before wrapping in freezer paper or polythene.

Scones, Baps, Drop Scones, Crumpets, Fruit Tarts, Cakes and home-made Jam for a farmhouse tea can all be stored in the freezer (see recipes pp. 62, 140, 141, 148).

Variety breads baked and frozen, then thawed for a special occasion.

The dough should be thawed in a moist warm place, quickly. Speed will help to give a light-textured loaf. After thawing the dough can be shaped and proved again before baking. Shaped bread and rolls should only be proved once, in a warm place, before baking.

Biscuits

Biscuits are the exception to the rule that cooked frozen goods are better than uncooked ones. Baked biscuits do freeze very well, but they store equally well in tins, so there is no advantage in using valuable freezer space for them. The most useful and time-saving way of preparing biscuits is to freeze batches of any favourite recipe in cylinder shapes, wrapped in freezer paper, polythene or foil. Overwrapping is advisable to avoid dents in the freezer from other packages. The dough will be all the better for having been frozen, giving light crisp biscuits. To use, leave in freezer wrappings in the refrigerator for 45 minutes until just beginning to soften, then cut in slices and bake; if the dough gets too soft it will be difficult to cut. If baked biscuits are to be stored, they must be carefully packed in layers in cartons with Cellophane or greaseproof paper between layers and with crumpled up paper in air spaces to safeguard freshness and stop breakages.

Icings and Fillings

Cakes for storage should not be filled with cream, jam or fruit. Butter icings are best, but an iced cake must be absolutely firm before wrapping and freezing. Brief chilling in the refrigerator will achieve this in hot weather. Wrappings must be removed before thawing to allow moisture to escape and to avoid smudging the icing. If sponge or flavoured cakes are to be packed for future icing later on, the layers can be stacked with Cellophane, foil or greaseproof paper between them, and can be separated easily for filling when thawed.

Flavourings and Decorations

Flavourings must be pure for all icings and fillings, and vanilla extract or vanilla sugar should be used when vanilla is needed. Highly spiced foods may develop off-flavours, so spice cakes should not usually be frozen, though an ordinary gingerbread is perfectly satisfactory. Chocolate, coffee, and fruit-flavoured cakes freeze very well. There is no particular advantage in decorating cakes before they are frozen, and nuts, coloured balls, grated chocolate etc. should be put on when the cake is fully thawed, just before serving; otherwise moisture may be absorbed and colour changes affect the appearance of the cake.

Preparation for Freezing Pastry

Short pastry and flaky pastry freeze equally well either cooked or uncooked, but a standard balanced recipe should be used for best results. Commercially-frozen pastry is one of the most useful and successful freezer stand-bys. Pastry can be stored unbaked or baked; baked pastry keeps longer (baked: 6 months; unbaked: 4 months), but unbaked pastry has a better flavour and scent, and is crisper and flakier.

Unbaked Pastry

Pastry can be rolled, formed into a square, wrapped in greaseproof paper, then in foil or

Scones with desserts and pastries finished with commercially frozen cream.

Frozen vol-au-vents and ice cream make this party dessert.

polythene for freezing. This pastry takes time to thaw, and may crumble when rolled. It should be thawed slowly, then cooked as fresh pastry and eaten fresh-baked, *not* returned to the freezer in cooked form.

Baked Pastry

Flan cases, patty cases and vol-au-vent cases are all useful to keep ready-baked. For storage, it is best to keep them in the cases in which they are baked or in foil cases. Small cases can be packed in boxes in layers with paper between. Baked cases should be thawed in their wrappings at room temperature before filling. They can be heated in a low oven if a hot filling is to be used.

Preparation for Freezing Pies

Frozen pies provide useful meals, and are a neat way of storing surplus fruit, meat and poultry. Large pies can be stored, also turnovers, pasties and individual fruit pies. Both pies and flans can be stored baked or unbaked. A baked pie usually keeps longer (depending on the filling), but an unbaked pie has a better flavour and scent, and the pastry is crisper and flakier. Almost all fillings can be used, except those with custard which separates. Meringue toppings should not be used as they toughen and dry during storage.

You can freeze pies with unbaked or baked pastry.

Baked Pies

Pies can be baked in the normal way, then cooled quickly before freezing. A pie is best prepared and frozen in foil, but can be stored in a rust-proof and crack-proof container. The container should be put into freezer paper or polythene for freezing. A cooked pie should be heated at 375° F, 190° C, Gas Mark 5, for 40–50 minutes for a double-crust pie and for 30–50 minutes for a one-crust pie, depending on size. Cooked pies can also be thawed in their wrappings at room temperature and eaten without reheating.

Unbaked Pies

Pies can be prepared with or without a bottom crust. To prevent sogginess, it is better to freeze unbaked pies before wrapping them. Air vents should be cut in the top crust after freezing, not before. To bake pies, cut slits in the frozen top crust and bake unthawed like fresh pies, allowing about 10 minutes longer than the normal cooking time.

Fruit Fillings

If the surface of the bottom crust of fruit pies is brushed with egg white, it will not get soggy. Fruit pies can be made with cooked or uncooked fillings. Apples tend to brown if stored in a pie for more than 4 weeks, even if treated with lemon juice, so it is better to combine frozen pastry and frozen apples to make a pie.

If time is likely to be short, it is often convenient to freeze ready-made fruit pie fillings ahead, ready to fit into fresh pastry when needed; this is also a good way of freezing surplus fruit in a handy form. The mixture is best frozen in a sponge-cake tin or an oven-glass pie plate lined with foil, then removed from container and wrapped in foil for storage; the same container can then be used for making the pie later on. A little cornflour or flaked tapioca added to fruit when cooking it gives a firm pie filling which cuts well and does not seep through the pastry.

Pastry made into pasties and frozen when baked.

Meat Fillings

Meat pies can be completely cooked so that they need only be reheated for serving. Preparation time is saved however if the meat filling is cooked and cooled, then topped with pastry. If the pie is made in this form, the time taken to cook the pastry is enough to heat the meat filling, and the process takes only a little longer than heating the whole pie.

Pies are most easily frozen in foil containers which can be used in the oven for final cooking. If a bottom crust is used, sogginess will be prevented if the bottom pastry is brushed with melted butter or lard just before filling. Pies should be reheated at 400° F, 200° C, Gas Mark 6, for the required time, according to size; they should not be stored longer than 2 months.

Hot Water Crust Pies

These are normally eaten cold, and can be frozen baked or unbaked; but there are obvious risks attached to freezing them. The pastry is made with hot water, and the pie must be completely baked *and cooled* before freezing; and the jelly must only be added just before the pie is to be served. The easiest way to do this is to freeze the stock separately at the time of making the pie, and when the pie is thawing (which takes about 4 hours) the partially-thawed pie can be filled with boiling stock through the hole in the crust (which will speed up the thawing process). Another method involves freezing the pie unbaked, partially thawing it and then baking it. However, this means that the uncooked meat is in contact with the warm uncooked pastry during the making process, and unless the pie is very carefully handled while cooling, there is every risk of dangerous organisms entering the meat.

It seems better therefore to avoid freezing game or pork pies made with this type of pastry.

Open Tarts

Tarts with only a bottom crust can be filled and frozen very successfully. They are better frozen before wrapping to avoid spoiling the surface of the filling during packing.

Pizza

Bought or home-made pizza can be frozen, and are useful for entertaining and for snack meals. The pizza is best frozen on a flat foil plate on which it can be baked, wrapped in foil for storage. Anchovies should be omitted from the topping if possible as their saltiness may cause rancidity in the fatty cheese during storage; they can be added at the reheating stage. Fresh herbs should be used rather than dried. To serve, unwrap and thaw at room temperature for 1 hour, then bake at 375° F, 190° C, Gas Mark 5, for 25 minutes, and serve very hot.

Quiches

Open savoury flans or quiches made with short pastry are best completed and baked before freezing. They should be frozen without wrapping to avoid spoiling the surface, then wrapped in foil or polythene for storage, or packed in boxes to avoid damage. It is easier to bake and freeze these flans in foil cases, but this does not give much depth of filling, so that it is preferable to prepare them in flan rings, freeze unwrapped, and pack in boxes to avoid breaking the sides. They should be thawed in loose wrappings at room temperature to serve cold, but taste better if reheated. The traditional Quiche Lorraine freezes well, and spinach, shellfish and mushroom flans are also good. Leftover meat, fish or vegetables can also be bound with a savoury sauce and frozen in a pastry case.

Flan Cases

Unfilled flan cases can be frozen baked or unbaked. Unbaked cases should be frozen in flan rings. Baked cases are fragile, and are best packed in boxes to avoid crushing. Baked cases are the most useful to keep in the freezer as a meal can be produced more quickly with them. Baked cases should be thawed in their wrappings at room temperature before filling (about 1 hour should be enough); but a hot filling can be used when the case is taken from the freezer and the whole flan then heated in a slow oven.

Flans

Filled flans with open tops are best completed and baked before freezing, whether they are savoury or sweet. They should be frozen without wrapping to avoid spoiling the surface, then wrapped in foil or polythene for storage, or packed in boxes to avoid damage. Custard fillings should be avoided; so should meringue toppings which toughen and dry during storage. A meringue topping can be added just before serving. Thaw flans in loose wrappings at room temperature for 2 hours to serve cold, or reheat if required. Storage time: 2 months with fresh fillings; 1 month if made with leftover meat or vegetables.

Preparation for Freezing Sandwiches

Every filling keeps for a different length of time; so the best general rule is not to store any sandwiches in the freezer for longer than 4 weeks. Sandwiches should be packaged in

Frozen salmon in triple-decker sandwiches toasted after thawing.

groups of six or eight rather than individually; an extra slice or crust of bread at each end of the package will help to prevent them drying out.

Avoid fillings which contain cooked egg whites, which become dry and tough with freezing. Also avoid raw vegetables such as celery, lettuce, tomatoes and carrots, and salad cream or mayonnaise which will curdle and separate when frozen and soak into the bread when thawed. To prevent fillings seeping through, butter the bread liberally; this is easier to do if the bread is one day old.

Give variety to sandwiches by using a number of breads. Whole wheat, rye, pumpernickel and fruit breads are all excellent (the brown breads are particularly good for fish fillings, and the fruit bread for cheese and sweet fillings).

Sandwiches should not be frozen against the freezer wall as it will result in uneven thawing. Put the packages a few inches from the wall of the freezer, and see that the crusty edges of the sandwiches are towards the wall. Sandwiches should be defrosted in their wrappings at room temperature for four hours.

When quantities of sandwiches must be prepared, an assembly-line technique will speed up matters. Try doing them this way:
(a) Soften butter or margarine (but do not melt).
(b) Prepare fillings and refrigerate ready for use.
(c) Assemble wrapping materials.
(d) Assemble breads and cut (or split rolls or baps).
(e) Spread bread slices, going right to the edge to prevent fillings soaking in.
(f) Spread fillings evenly on bread to ensure even thawing time.

(g) Close and stack sandwiches.

(h) Cut with a sharp knife (sandwiches are best left in rather large portions, such as half slices) and leave crusts on.

(i) Wrap sandwiches tightly in Cellophane, then in foil or other moisture-vapour-proof wrap. With an inner wrapping, the other covering may be removed and retained at home and the neat inner package taken in a lunch box for thawing.

(j) Label and freeze.

These fillings are very satisfactory:

Cheese   Cream cheese with olives and peanuts

Cream cheese with chutney

Cream cheese with chopped dates, figs or prunes

Cottage cheese with orange marmalade or apricot jam

Blue cheese with roast beef

Blue cheese with chopped cooked bacon

Cheddar cheese and chopped olives or chutney

Fish   Mashed sardines, hard-boiled egg yolk and a squeeze of lemon juice

Minced shrimps, crab or lobster with cream cheese and lemon juice

Tuna with chutney

Canned salmon with cream cheese and lemon juice

Meat and Poultry   Sliced meat such as tongue, corned beef, luncheon meat and chutney

Sliced roast beef with horseradish sauce

Sliced roast lamb with mint jelly

Sliced chicken or turkey with ham and chutney

Minced ham with chopped pickled cucumber and cream cheese

Open Freezing Baked Goods

It is preferable to freeze iced cakes and delicate pies before packaging them. They can be frozen on metal or plastic trays, and then packed in polythene or foil, or in a rigid box to prevent crushing.

Here are notes on preparing, packing, storing and cooking various baked goods:

Babas and Savarins

Preparation   (a) If syrup has been poured on to cake, pack in leakproof container.
(b) Pack cake without syrup in foil or polythene.

Serving   (a) Thaw (without wrappings) at room temperature. (b) Thaw without wrappings at room temperature, and pour on warm syrup.
High Quality Storage Life   3 months

Biscuits

Preparation   (a) Make dough and form into cylinder about 2 in. diameter. Wrap in foil or polythene. (b) Bake biscuits. Pack carefully in boxes to avoid crushing. Biscuits keep well in tins, so freezer space need not be wasted.

Serving   (a) Thaw in wrappings in refrigerator for 45 minutes. Cut in slices and bake at 375°F, 190°C, Gas Mark 5, for 10 minutes. (b) Thaw in wrappings at room temperature for 1 hour. Baked biscuits may be rather soft when thawed.
High Quality Storage Life   (a) 2 months, (b) 4 months

Bread (Baked)

Preparation   Wrap in foil or polythene bags.

Serving   (a) Thaw in wrappings at room temperature for 3–6 hours, or in refrigerator overnight. (b) Put frozen loaf in foil in moderate oven (400°F, 200°C or Gas Mark 6) for 45 minutes.
High Quality Storage Life   4 weeks (plain bread); 6 weeks (enriched bread); 1 week (crisp-crusted bread).

Bread Dough

Preparation   (a) Form kneaded dough into a ball. Put in lightly greased polythene bag. Seal tightly and freeze at once. (b) Put dough in a large lightly greased polythene bag; tie loosely at top and leave to rise. Turn on to floured surface, knock back and knead until firm. Replace in polythene bag, seal tightly and freeze at once.

Serving   Unseal bag, and tie loosely at the top to allow space for rising. Thaw 6 hours at room temperature or overnight in refrigerator. Knock back, shape, rise and bake.
High Quality Storage Life   (a) 8 weeks (plain dough); 5 weeks (enriched dough); (b) 3 weeks.

Bread (Fruit and Nut)

Preparation   Do not overbake. Cool quickly. Pack in polythene bags.

Serving   Thaw in wrappings at room temperature. Slice while partly frozen to prevent crumbling.
High Quality Storage Life   2 months

Bread (Part-baked)

Preparation Leave in wrapper and put into polythene bag. Seal and freeze at once.

Serving Put frozen loaf in hot oven (425°F, 220°C or Gas Mark 7) for 30 minutes. Cool 2 hours before cutting.
High Quality Storage Life 4 months

Bread (Sliced)

Preparation Leave in wrapper and put in polythene bags. Seal and freeze at once.

Serving (a) Thaw in wrappings at room temperature for 3–6 hours, or in refrigerator overnight. (b) Separate frozen slices with a knife and toast at once.
High Quality Storage Life 4 weeks

Brioche

Preparation Pack immediately after baking and cooling in polythene bags.

Serving Thaw in wrappings at room temperature for 30 minutes, and heat in oven or under grill, with or without filling.
High Quality Storage Life 2 months

Cake (Butter-iced)

Preparation Put together cake layers with butter icing, and ice top with butter icing. Do not add decorations. Fast-freeze on a tray without wrappings. When frozen, pack in box, or in foil or polythene bag.

Serving Remove wrappings and thaw at room temperature for 1½ hours. Add decorations.
High Quality Storage Life 4 months

Cake (Light Fruit)

Preparation A light fruit cake, such as Dundee or sultana cake, will freeze well. Wrap in foil or polythene bag.

Serving Thaw in wrappings at room temperature for 2 hours.
High Quality Storage Life 4 months

Cake (Sponge)

Preparation Sponges made with and without fat freeze equally well. Pack in layers with greaseproof paper or Cellophane between. Pack in foil or polythene bag.

Serving Thaw in wrappings at room temperature for 1½ hours.
High Quality Storage Life 4 months (with fat); 10 months (fatless).

Cakes (Slab)

Preparation Light fruit cakes, flavoured cakes (e.g. chocolate), gingerbread and spicecakes may be frozen in their baking tins, wrapped in foil or polythene.

Serving Thaw in wrappings at room temperature for 1½ hours. Ice if required and cut in pieces.
High Quality Storage Life 4 months (fruit and flavoured); 2 months (ginger and spice).

Cakes (Small)

Preparation Cakes made in bun tins, paper or foil cases can be frozen plain or iced. (a) Pack plain cakes in usable quantities in polythene bags. (b) Pack iced cakes in boxes layered with greaseproof paper or Cellophane. Iced cakes are best fast-frozen on tray before packing.

Serving (a) Thaw in wrappings at room temperature for 1 hour. (b) Remove wrappings and thaw at room temperature for 1 hour.
High Quality Storage Life 4 months

Cake (Rich Fruit)

Preparation This type of cake will keep well in a tin, so freezer space should not be wasted. If a rich fruit cake is to be frozen, wrap in foil or polythene bag.

Serving Thaw in wrappings at room temperature for 2 hours.
High Quality Storage Life 10 months

Choux Pastry, Éclairs and Cream Buns

Preparation (a) Bake éclairs or cream buns. Freeze without filling or icing. Pack in boxes or bags. (b) Fill cases with ice cream. Freeze unwrapped on trays. Pack in boxes.

Serving (a) Thaw in wrappings at room temperature for 2 hours. Fill and ice. (b) Thaw at room temperature for 10 minutes. Pour over chocolate or toffee sauce.
High Quality Storage Life 1 month

Croissants

Preparation   Pack immediately after baking and cooling. Pack in bags, or in boxes to avoid crushing and flaking.

Serving   Thaw in wrappings at room temperature for 30 minutes, and heat in oven or under grill.
High Quality Storage Life   2 months

Crumpets

Preparation   Pack in usable quantities in polythene bags.

Serving   Thaw in wrappings at room temperature for 30 minutes, then toast.
High Quality Storage Life   10 months

Danish Pastries

Preparation   Prepare un-iced or with a light water icing. Pack in foil trays with lids, or in boxes to prevent crushing.

Serving   Remove wrappings and thaw at room temperature for 1 hour. Heat lightly if liked.
High Quality Storage Life   2 months

Doughnuts

Preparation   Ring doughnuts freeze better than jam doughnuts which may become soggy. Drain well from fat, and do not roll in sugar. Pack in polythene bags.

Serving   Heat frozen doughnuts at 400°F, 200°C, Gas Mark 6 for 8 minutes, then roll in sugar.
High Quality Storage Life   1 month

Drop Scones

Preparation   Cool thoroughly before packing. Pack in boxes, foil or bags.

Serving   Thaw in wrappings at room temperature for 1 hour.
High Quality Storage Life   2 months

Muffins

Preparation   Pack in usable quantities in polythene bags.

Serving   Thaw in wrappings at room temperature for 30 minutes, then toast.
High Quality Storage Life   10 months

Pancakes

Preparation Cool thoroughly before packing. Put layers of greaseproof paper or Cellophane between large thin pancakes. Wrap in foil or polythene.

Serving Thaw in wrappings at room temperature and separate. Heat in low oven, or on a plate over steam, covered with a cloth.
High Quality Storage Life 2 months

Pastry (Slab)

Preparation Roll pastry, form into a square and in greaseproof paper. Overwrap in foil or polythene. Pack in usable quantities (i.e. 8 oz or 1 lb.).

Serving Thaw at room temperature for 2 hours. Eat freshly baked.
High Quality Storage Life 4 months

Pastry Cases

Preparation Make up flan cases, patty cases and vol-au-vent cases. Use foil containers if possible. (a) Freeze unbaked cases packed in foil or polythene. (b) Bake cases and pack in boxes to prevent crushing.

Serving Thaw unbaked cases at room temperature for 1 hour before baking. (a) Thaw baked cases at room temperature before filling. (b) Put hot filling into frozen cases and heat in oven.
High Quality Storage Life 4 months

Rolls and Buns

Preparation Pack in polythene bags in usable quantities. Seal and freeze at once.

Serving (a) Thaw in wrappings at room temperature for $1\frac{1}{2}$ hours. (b) Put frozen rolls or buns in foil in a hot oven (450°F, 230°C or Gas Mark 8) for 15 minutes.
High Quality Storage Life 4 weeks

Rolls (Part-baked)

Preparation Leave in wrapper and put into polythene bag. Seal and freeze at once.

Serving Put frozen rolls in moderate oven (400°F, 200°C or Gas Mark 6) for 15 minutes.
High Quality Storage Life 4 months

Freshly-baked rolls stored in the freezer can be quickly heated for use.

Sandwiches

Preparation   Avoid fillings of cooked egg whites, salad dressings, mayonnaise, raw vegetables or jam. Spread bread with butter. Pack in groups of six or eight sandwiches, with an extra crust at each end to prevent drying out. Keep crusts on, and do not cut sandwiches in pieces. Wrap in foil or polythene and seal tightly.

Serving   (a) Thaw in wrappings in refrigerator for 12 hours, or at room temperature for 4 hours. Trim crusts and cut in pieces. (b) Put frozen sandwiches under grill to thaw while toasting.
High Quality Storage Life   1 month

Sandwiches (Open)

Preparation   Butter bread thickly. Make up without salad garnishes, open freeze and pack in single layer in rigid plastic box.

Serving   Thaw at room temperature for 2 hours. Garnish with salad and dressings.
High Quality Storage Life   1 week

Sandwiches (Pinwheel, Club and Ribbon)

Preparation   Prepare but do not cut in pieces. Wrap tightly in foil.

Serving   Thaw in wrappings in refrigerator for 12 hours, or at room temperature for 4 hours. Cut in pieces.
High Quality Storage Life   1 month

Sandwiches (Rolled)

Preparation   Flatten bread with rolling pin to ease rolling. Butter well and wrap around filling. Pack closely together in box to prevent unrolling.

Serving   Thaw in wrappings in refrigerator for 12 hours, or at room temperature for 4 hours.
High Quality Storage Life   1 month

Scones

Preparation   Pack in usable quantities in polythene bags.

Serving   (a) Thaw in wrappings at room temperature for 1 hour. (b) Heat frozen scones (with a covering of foil) at 350°F, 180°C, Gas Mark 4 for 10 minutes.
High Quality Storage Life   2 months

Yeast

Preparation   Weigh into $\frac{1}{4}$ oz, $\frac{1}{2}$ oz or 1 oz cubes. Wrap cubes in polythene and label carefully. Pack in box.

Serving   Thaw 30 minutes at room temperature. Frozen yeast may be grated coarsely for immediate use.
High Quality Storage Life   12 months

Waffles

Preparation   Do not brown too much. Cool and pack in usable quantities.

Serving   Heat frozen waffles under grill or in oven until crisp.
High Quality Storage Life   2 months

Here are some good pastry recipes to store in your freezer:

White Bread

$2\frac{1}{2}$ *lb white bread flour*
1 oz fresh yeast
2 oz fat (butter, lard or margarine)
$\frac{1}{2}$ oz salt
$1\frac{1}{2}$ pints warm water

Warm a large bowl and put in flour. Make a well in centre and sprinkle salt round edge. Cream yeast with a little warm water and pour into the well. Add remaining water and warmed fat and mix well to a consistency like putty. Leave to prove until double its size. Divide into loaf tins and leave to prove again until bread reaches top of tins. Bake at 450°F, 230°C, Gas Mark 8, for 45 minutes, turning bread once in the oven. Cool on a rack and leave overnight. Pack in polythene bags or in heavy duty foil.

To serve
Thaw in wrappings at room temperature for 3 hours.
High Quality Storage Life   8–12 months

Baps

1 lb white bread flour
2 oz lard
1 level teaspoon sugar
2 level teaspoons salt
1 oz yeast
½ pint lukewarm milk
 and water

Sieve the flour and rub in the lard and sugar. Dissolve the salt in half the liquid, and cream the yeast into the rest of the liquid. Mix into the flour, knead and prove until double in size. Divide into pieces and make into small flat rounds about 4 ins. across. Brush with milk, put on a greased baking sheet, prove again, and bake at 450°F, 230°C, Gas Mark 8, for 20 minutes. Cool on a rack. Pack in polythene bags. Baps may be split, buttered and filled before freezing.

To serve
Thaw in wrappings at room temperature for 1 hour.
High Quality Storage Life   Unfilled: 10–12 months. Filled: 1 month.

Drop Scones

8 oz plain white flour
¼ level teaspoon salt
½ level teaspoon
 bicarbonate of soda
1 level teaspoon cream
 of tartar
1 level tablespoon sugar
1 egg
¼ pint milk

Sieve together flour, salt, soda and cream of tartar. Stir in sugar and mix to a batter with egg and milk. Cook in spoonfuls on lightly greased griddle or frying pan. When bubbles appear on the surface, turn quickly and cook other side. Cool in a cloth to keep soft. Pack in foil, with a sheet of Cellophane or greaseproof paper between layers.

To serve
Thaw at room temperature for 1 hour, and butter.
High Quality Storage Life   2 months

Basic Scones

1 lb plain white flour
1 teaspoon bicarbonate of soda
2 teaspoons cream of tartar
3 oz butter
¼ pint milk

Sift together flour, soda and cream of tartar and rub in butter until mixture is like breadcrumbs. Mix with milk to soft dough. Roll out, cut in rounds, and place close together on greased baking sheet. Bake at 450°F, 230°C, Gas Mark 8, for 12 minutes. Cool.
Fruit Scones   Add 1½ oz sugar and 2 oz dried fruit.
Cheese Scones   Add pinch each of salt and pepper and 3 oz grated cheese. Pack in sixes or dozens in polythene bags.

To serve
Thaw in wrappings at room temperature for 1 hour, or heat at 350°F, 180°C, Gas Mark 4, for 10 minutes with a covering of foil.
High Quality Storage Life   2 months

Croissants

1 oz butter
¼ pint warm milk
1 heaped teaspoon salt
1½ tablespoons sugar
1 oz fresh yeast dissolved in a little warm water
12 oz white bread flour
4 oz butter
1 egg yolk beaten with a little milk

Put butter in bowl, pour on warm milk and add salt and sugar. Cool to lukewarm, then add yeast and gradually add flour to give a soft dough. Cover dough with damp cloth and leave for 2 hours. Knead dough, chill thoroughly, and roll into a rectangle. Spread butter lightly and evenly over dough. Fold over dough to a rectangle and roll again. Chill, roll and fold twice more at intervals of 30 minutes. Roll dough out to ¼ in. thickness and cut into 4 in. squares. Divide each square into 2 triangles, and roll each triangle up, starting at longest edge and rolling towards the point. Bend into crescent shapes, put on floured baking sheet, brush with beaten egg and milk, and bake at 425°F, 220°C, Gas Mark 7, for 15 minutes. Cool. Pack into polythene bags. Store carefully.

To serve
Thaw in wrappings at room temperature for 30 minutes, then lightly heat in the oven or under the grill.
High Quality Storage Life   2 months

Basic Pancakes

4 oz plain flour
¼ teaspoon salt
1 egg and 1 egg yolk
½ pint milk
1 tablespoon oil or
    melted butter

Sift flour and salt and mix in egg and egg yolk and a little milk. Work together and gradually add remaining milk, beating to a smooth batter. Fold in oil or melted butter. Fry large or small thin pancakes. Pack in layers separated by Cellophane and put in foil or polythene bag.

To serve
Separate the pancakes, put on a baking sheet and cover with foil, and heat at 400°F, 200°C, Gas Mark 6, for 10 minutes, or thaw and use cold with ice cream filling.
High Quality Storage Life   2 months

Mincemeat Pinwheel Buns

Yeast Liquid:
*Blend ½ oz fresh yeast in
    1/8th pint water OR
    dissolve 1 teaspoon
    sugar in ½ pint warm
    water and sprinkle
    2 level teaspoons
    dried yeast on top.
    Leave until frothy,
    about 10 minutes.*

**Other Dough
Ingredients:**
*8 oz plain flour
1 level teaspoon salt
1 tablespoon caster sugar
1 beaten egg
Grated rind and juice of
    ½ orange*

Filling:
*4 tablespoons
    mincemeat
4 oz peeled, cored and
    coarsely grated
    cooking apples*

Glaze:
*2 tablespoons clear
    honey*

Prepare yeast liquid. Mix yeast liquid with other dough ingredients and work to a firm dough. Turn out and knead well on a floured surface until dough feels smooth and elastic. Put dough to rise in a large, lightly-oiled polythene bag, loosely tied at the top, until doubled in size, about 1 hour in a warm place. Turn out risen dough and knead lightly for 2 minutes. Roll out to an oblong 6 by 12 in. Mix together mincemeat and grated apple and spread on dough. Roll up lengthwise like a Swiss roll. Cut into ½-in. slices and place in greased bun tins. Place tins inside a large, oiled polythene bag and leave to rise until doubled in size, about 30 minutes in a warm place. Remove polythene and bake at 200° C (400° F) Gas Mark 6 for 20–30 minutes until golden-brown. Brush with honey while still warm and cool on a cooling rack. Freeze unglazed. Cool and wrap tightly in heavy duty foil. Label. Makes 24 buns.

To serve
Place frozen buns, wrapped in foil, in a hot oven, 200° C (400° F) Gas Mark 6 for 10–15 minutes. Brush with honey glaze and cool.
High Quality Storage Life   3 months

Thin pancakes with the traditional accompaniment of lemon and sugar.

Christmas Candle Ring

Yeast Liquid:
Blend ½ oz fresh yeast in ¼ pint warm milk plus 4 tablespoons water OR dissolve 1 level teaspoon caster sugar in ¼ pint warm milk and 4 tablespoons water and sprinkle on 2 level teaspoons dried yeast, and leave until frothy, about 10 minutes.

Other ingredients:
1 lb plain flour
1 level teaspoon salt
2 oz margarine or butter

Filling:
3 oz crystallised orange slices
2 oz crystallised pineapple
1 oz blanched almonds
1 oz soft brown sugar
½ teaspoon cinnamon

Egg Wash:
Blend 1 beaten egg with 1 level teaspoon sugar and 1 tablespoon water

Decoration
4 oz icing sugar
1 tablespoon water
1 slice crystallised orange
Candle and holly leaves

Prepare yeast liquid. Then mix flour and salt and rub in fat. Add yeast liquid and work to a firm dough until sides of bowl are clean. Turn dough out on to a lightly floured surface and knead thoroughly until firm and elastic and no longer sticky, about 10 minutes. Shape dough into a ball and place in a large, lightly oiled polythene bag, loosely tied at the top. Leave to rise until dough is double in size and springs back when pressed gently with a floured finger, about 1 hour in a warm place, 2 hours at average room temperature. Turn risen dough on to a lightly floured surface and knead until dough is firm, about 2 minutes. Divide dough into 2 and roll out each piece to a long rectangle about 12 by 5 in.

For filling, chop orange, pineapple and almonds and mix with brown sugar and cinnamon. Spread filling on both pieces of dough. Twist both pieces of dough together, shape into a circle and seal ends. Place on a greased baking tray, with a dariole mould in the centre, brush with egg wash and cover with oiled polythene. Leave to rise until double in size, about ½–¾ hour in a warm place. Remove polythene and bake at 200° C (400° F) Gas Mark 6 for 40–45 minutes until golden-brown, and loaf sounds hollow when tapped underneath. Cool. Freeze without icing, wrapped in heavy duty foil. Seal tightly and label.

To serve
Place frozen loaf, wrapped in foil in a hot oven, 200° C (400° F) Gas Mark 6 for 30 minutes. Cool in foil. Ice as below.
To decorate for immediate use, mix icing sugar with water to form a glacé icing and spoon over bread. Cut crystallised orange slice into 6 triangles and place on top of icing. Place candle in dariole mould and surround with holly.
High Quality Storage Life   3 months

Traditional Christmas baking: Christmas Candle Ring, Stollen and Mincemeat Pinwheel Buns
(see recipes pp. 142, 144, 146).

Stollen

Batter Ingredients:
2 oz plain flour
½ level teaspoon sugar
½ oz fresh yeast OR 1
    level teaspoon dried
    yeast
4 oz warm milk

Other Ingredients:
2 oz butter
2 oz caster sugar
1 beaten egg
6 oz plain flour
½ level teaspoon salt
3 oz raisins
2 oz quartered glacé
    cherries
1 oz mixed peel
1 oz chopped almonds
Grated rind of ½ lemon
½ oz melted butter

Decoration:
Sifted icing sugar

Mix batter ingredients in a large bowl and set aside until frothy, about 20–30 minutes in a warm place. Cream butter and sugar, add egg and beat well. Add to the yeast batter with all the remaining ingredients, except the melted butter. Mix well together to make a soft dough. Place bowl in a large, lightly oiled polythene bag. Leave to rise until double in size, about 1½ hours in a warm place. Turn dough on to a lightly floured board and knead well, for about 10 minutes, until smooth and elastic. Roll out to an oval about 10 by 8 in., brush with melted butter and fold over lengthwise so that the top layer is 1 in. from the edge of the bottom. Place stollen on a greased baking sheet and cover with oiled polythene. Leave to rise until doubled in size and dough springs back when pressed with a floured finger, about ½–¾ hour in a warm place. Remove polythene and bake at 190° C (375° F) Gas Mark 5 for 30–35 minutes until golden-brown. Cool. Freeze without icing sugar, wrapped tightly in heavy duty foil. Label.

To serve
Place frozen stollen wrapped in foil in a hot oven, 200° C (400° F) Gas Mark 6 for 25–30 minutes. Cool in foil. Dust with icing sugar before serving.
High Quality Storage Life   3 months

Chocolate Fudge Cake

4 oz butter
2 tablespoons golden
    syrup
8 oz crushed sweet
    biscuits
1 oz stoned raisins
2 oz quartered glacé
    cherries
5 oz plain chocolate
Chocolate peppermint
    creams and ice cream
    or fudge icing

Fudge Icing
2 oz chocolate
1 oz butter
6 oz icing sugar

Grease and base-line a 1-lb. loaf or round tin. Melt butter and syrup in a saucepan. Stir in biscuits, fruit and melted or chopped plain chocolate. Press firmly into prepared tin and leave in a cool place to set. Later turn out on to a board. Either top with chocolate peppermint creams, grill for 1 minute, then top with ice cream, or ice. For the fudge icing, melt chocolate and butter with 3 dessertspoonfuls of water, over a gentle heat. Remove from heat. Stir in sifted icing sugar and beat until cool and thick. Spread icing over cake. Freeze on an open tray, and wrap in foil or polythene for storage.

To serve
Thaw at room temperature for 2 hours. If preferred, the cake can be frozen without icing, which can be added after thawing.
High Quality Storage Life 2 months

Chocolate Fudge Cake, Walnut Brownies and Feather Squares.

Walnut Brownies

6 oz margarine
2 level tablespoons
  cocoa
6 oz caster sugar
2 eggs
2 oz plain flour
2 oz chopped walnuts

Melt 2 oz margarine, stir in the cocoa and set aside. Cream the remaining butter with the sugar until lighter in colour and texture, and gradually beat in the eggs. Fold in the sieved flour; add the walnuts and cocoa mixture. Turn into a greased and base-lined 7-in. tin and bake in a moderate oven, 350°F, 180°C, Gas Mark 4, for approximately 45 minutes. Leave to cool in the tin. Turn out and wrap in foil or polythene to freeze.

To serve
Thaw at room temperature and sprinkle with caster sugar, or cover with melted plain chocolate. Cut in squares.
High Quality Storage Life 2 months

Feather Squares

3 large eggs
3 oz caster sugar
3 oz plain flour
1 level tablespoon cocoa

Filling
4 oz plain chocolate
½ pint double cream
½ teaspoon vanilla
  essence

Icing
2 oz plain chocolate
A knob of butter
1 heaped tablespoon
  sifted icing sugar
1 oz plain chocolate,
  melted

Whisk eggs and sugar, in a bowl placed over a pan of hot water, until thick and creamy. Fold in sifted flour and cocoa and pour mixture into a greased and base-lined 12 × 8 in. tin. Bake in a hot oven, 400°F, 200°C, Gas Mark 6, for 15 minutes, or until cooked. Cool on a wire rack. Slice in half for the filling. Place the 4 oz chocolate in a pan with the cream and heat gently until melted, stirring continuously. Pour into a bowl and refrigerate for at least an hour. Add vanilla essence and beat to a mousse-like texture. Spread thickly over one piece of cake and lift the other on top. Freeze on an open tray, and wrap in foil or polythene for storage.

To serve
Thaw at room temperature for 2 hours, and ice. For the icing, melt chocolate and butter together in a basin over hot water and leave until melted. Beat in the icing sugar and 1 tablespoonful warm water, until smooth. Spread over the top of the cake. Cut into squares or slices. Place the chocolate in a greaseproof paper piping bag, cut off the tip and pipe zig-zag lines over the top of each slice.
High Quality Storage Life 2 months

Light Cream Chocolate Cake

4 eggs
4½ oz caster sugar
2½ oz plain flour
1 oz drinking chocolate
  powder
¼ pint double cream

Whip the eggs and sugar together until light and fluffy. Carefully fold in the flour and drinking chocolate powder sifted together. Bake in two 7-in. greased sponge tins at 400° F (200° C) Gas Mark 6 for 15 minutes. Cool on a wire cake tray. Whip the cream with about 1 tablespoon sugar, and use to sandwich the cakes together when they are quite cold. Open-freeze and wrap in polythene or foil.

To serve
Thaw at room temperature for 3 hours.
High Quality Storage Life 1 month.

148

Danish Pastries

8 oz white bread flour
½ level teaspoon salt
2½ oz sugar
½ oz yeast
¼ pint warm water
3 oz butter

Put flour and salt in a warm basin. Cream yeast with a little of the sugar and put into the flour together with the remaining sugar and water. Mix to a soft, slightly sticky dough, and leave to rise in a warm place until increased by one-third in volume. Form butter into a rectangle and dust with flour. Flatten dough with hands and fold with the fat in the centre like a parcel. Roll and fold twice like puff pastry. Leave in a cold place for 20 minutes, then roll and fold twice more and leave for 20 minutes. Roll out to ¼ in. thick. Fold squares of pastry over fillings of dried fruit, jam, marzipan or chopped nuts, to make envelope shapes. Brush pastries with a mixture of melted butter, milk and egg, and bake without proving at 375°F, 190°C, Gas Mark 5, for 30 minutes. Cool. The pastries may be frozen un-iced or with a light water icing. Pack in foil trays with foil lid, or put trays into polythene bags.

To serve
Thaw at room temperature, removing wrappings if iced, for 1 hour.
High Quality Storage Life 2 months

FREEZING COOKED DISHES

Cooked meals, and items which can be used straight from the freezer without further cooking are very useful. Strict hygiene must be observed in preparing cooked food for the freezer, and only fresh good-quality raw materials should be used. Cooked food must be cooled promptly and quickly by standing the container in cold water and ice cubes. Surplus fat should be removed after cooling and before freezing. Fried foods must be well drained on absorbent paper, and must be very cold before packing to avoid sogginess. Dishes such as pies, piped potatoes and decorated puddings should be frozen before wrapping to avoid damage to the surface of the food.

Preparation for Freezing Soup

Besides completed soups, meat, chicken and fish stock can all be frozen to use as a basis for fresh soups. These stocks should be strained, cooled and defatted, and packed into cartons with headspace. They are best thawed in a saucepan over low heat.

Soup which is thickened with ordinary flour tends to curdle on reheating, so cornflour is best as a thickening agent; it gives a creamy result. Rice flour can be used, but makes the soup glutinous. Porridge oats can be used for thicker meat soups. Starchy foods such as rice, pasta, barley and potatoes become slushy when frozen in liquid, and should only be added during the final reheating after freezing. It is also better to omit milk or cream from frozen soups, as results with these ingredients are variable; they, too, can be added when reheating.

Soup to be frozen should be cooled, and surplus fat removed as this will separate in storage and may cause off-flavours. Soup should be frozen in leak-proof containers, allowing $\frac{1}{2}$ in. headspace for wide-topped containers and $\frac{3}{4}$ in. headspace for narrow-topped containers. Rigid plastic containers are useful for storage; a very large quantity of soup can be frozen in a bread tin or in freezer boxes lined with foil; the solid block can then be wrapped in foil and stored like a brick.

Soup should not be stored for longer than 2 months. It will thicken during freezing, and allowance should be made for this in the recipe so that additional liquid can be added on reheating without spoiling the soup. Seasoning can cause off-flavours, so it is best to season after thawing. Clear soups can be heated in a saucepan over low heat, but cream soups should be heated in a double boiler and beaten well to keep them smooth.

Soup Garnishes

Herbs and croûtons can be frozen to give an attractive finish to soups, even when time is limited.

Herb Cubes

Herbs such as parsley and chives should be chopped and packed in ice cube trays with a little water, then each frozen cube wrapped in foil. The herb cubes can be reheated in the soup.

Croûtons and Cheese Croûtons

Croûtons can be prepared from lightly-toasted $\frac{1}{2}$ in. slices of bread which are then cut in cubes and dried out in an oven set at 350° F, 180° C, Gas Mark 4. They are best packed in small polythene bags and thawed in their wrappings at room temperature, but they can be reheated if preferred. As a variation, the bread can be toasted on one side only and the other side can be spread with grated cheese mixed with a little melted butter, egg yolk and seasoning; this is then toasted and the bread cut in cubes before packing.

Preparation for Freezing of Cooked Meat

Time can be saved by preparing meat dishes which can be frozen, then eaten cold or reheated after thawing. Pre-cooked joints, steaks and chops do not freeze successfully, since the outer surface sometimes develops an off-flavour, and reheating dries out the meat. Fried meats also tend to toughness, dryness and rancidity when frozen. Cold meat can however be frozen in slices, with or without sauce. Any combination dishes of meat and vegetables should include the vegetables when they are slightly undercooked, to avoid softness on reheating. In addition to casseroles and stews, good cooked dishes for freezing include cottage pie, galantines and meat loaves, meat balls, meat sauces, and meat pies. It is very important that all cooked meats should be cooled quickly before freezing. Where ingredients such as meat and gravy are to be combined, they should be thoroughly chilled separately before mixing; for instance hot gravy should not be poured over cold meat.

Preparation for Freezing of Cooked Poultry

Old birds such as boiling chickens are best if frozen when cooked, with the meat stripped from the bones. This meat can then be frozen or made at once into pies or casseroles, while the carcass can be simmered in the cooking liquid to make strong stock for freezing. Slices of cooked poultry can be frozen on their own or in a sauce (the latter is preferable to prevent drying out). If the meat is frozen without sauce, slices should be divided by sheets of Cellophane and then closely packed together to exclude air. Roast and fried poultry frozen to be eaten cold are not particularly successful; on thawing they tend to exude moisture and be flabby.

Sliced Meat and Poultry

Cold poached, boiled or steamed meat and poultry can well be frozen in slices to serve cold. Slices should be at least $\frac{1}{4}$ in. thick, separated by Cellophane or greaseproof paper, and must be packed tightly to avoid surfaces drying. They can then be put into cartons or bags. They should be thawed for 3 hours in a refrigerator in their container, then separated and placed on absorbent paper to remove any moisture. They are good; only ham and pork will lose colour when frozen like this.

A reheated freezer casserole of mince meat garnished with mashed potato when thawed.

A beef and vegetable casserole can be prepared, frozen and reheated in a foil container and accompanied by baked jacket potatoes, which also freeze well.

It is preferable to freeze meat and poultry slices in gravy or sauce to make them keep their juiciness. The liquid may be thickened with cornflour, and both the meat and the gravy or sauce should be cooled quickly, separately, before packing. These slices are best packaged in foil containers, covered with a lid, and this can save time in reheating as the container can go straight into the oven, keeping the meat moist. These frozen slices in gravy should be heated for 30 minutes at 350° F, 180° C, Gas Mark 4.

Casseroles

Casseroled meat and poultry is very useful to keep in the freezer. It is good sense to double the quantity of a casserole, using half when fresh and freezing the second half. For freezing, vegetables should be slightly undercooked in the casserole; pasta, rice, barley or potatoes should not be included or they will go slushy; onions, garlic and herbs should only be used sparingly, or should be added during reheating; sauces should be thickened with tomato purée, vegetable purée or cornflour, to avoid curdling on reheating. Oven-to-freezer casseroles can well be used if they are of the type advertised for the purpose, and they can be returned straight to the oven for reheating. Other oven-glass containers should be allowed to cool before placing in the freezer, and should be thawed before returning to the oven for serving. Casseroles and stews are very successful when frozen in foil containers which can be used in the oven, or in foil-lined containers so that the foil can be formed into a parcel for freezing, and the contents returned to the original container for heating and serving. If frozen in cartons, the dishes can be transferred to ovenware, or reheated in a double boiler, or even over direct heat if curdling is not likely to occur.

Galantines and Meat Loaves

Galantines are most easily used if cooked before freezing, ready to serve cold. They can be prepared directly in loaf tins, then turned out, wrapped and frozen. Meat loaves can be frozen uncooked. This is made easy if the mixture is packed into loaf tins lined with foil, the foil then being formed into a parcel for freezing; the frozen meat loaf can be returned to the original tin for baking.

For cold serving, any of these compact meats can be packed in slices, divided by Cellophane or greaseproof paper, and re-formed into a loaf shape for freezing. Slices can be separated while still frozen and thawed quickly on absorbent paper.

Pâtés

Pâtés made from liver, game or poultry, freeze extremely well. They can be packed in individual pots ready for serving, or cooked in loaf tins or terrines, then turned out and wrapped in foil for easy storage. Pâtés containing strong seasoning, herbs or garlic should be carefully overwrapped.

Any pâté which has exuded fat or excess juices during cooking must be carefully cooled and the excess fat or jelly scraped off before freezing. To serve, thaw small individual containers at room temperature for 1 hour. Thaw large pâtés in their wrappings in the refrigerator for 6 hours, or at room temperature for 3 hours, and use immediately after thawing. High quality storage life: 1 month. Pâtés can also be made with smoked fish, such as kippers or cod's roe. These are best prepared in small containers, well overwrapped. Any fish pâté should be thawed in a refrigerator for 3 hours, stirring occasionally to blend ingredients.

Cooked Fish

Fish should never be overcooked, and the time taken to reheat a cooked fish dish will not only spoil flavour and rob the fish of any nutritive value, but will also take as long as the original cooking. Leftover cooked fish can however be frozen in the form of a fish pie, fish cakes, or a ready-to-eat dish in sauce. Raw fish can be frozen, coated in batter or egg and breadcrumbs and fried; but it tends to go rancid, and will take about 15 minutes to reheat, so there is little advantage in freezing it.

Pasta

Pasta such as spaghetti and macaroni can be frozen successfully to be used with a variety of sauces. Composite meals such as macaroni cheese can also be frozen when cooked. Pasta shapes can be frozen to use with soup; but they should not be frozen in liquid as they become slushy, so are most conveniently added to the soup during the reheating period.

Pasta should be slightly undercooked, in boiling salted water. After thorough draining, it should be cooled under cold running water in a sieve, then shaken as dry as possible, packed into polythene bags, and frozen. To serve, the pasta is put into a pan of boiling water and brought back to the boil, then simmered until just tender, the time depending on the state in which it has been frozen. Composite dishes can be reheated in a double boiler or in the oven under a foil lid. High quality storage life: 1 month.

While it may not save much time to prepare pasta specially for the freezer, it is useful to be able to save excess quantities prepared for a meal, or to turn them into a composite dish for the freezer.

154

Sauces

Sweet and savoury sauces can well be frozen, and are useful for emergency meals. They can be in the form of complete sauces such as a meat sauce to use with spaghetti or rice, or you can freeze a basic white or brown sauce to be used with other ingredients when reheated. Sauces for freezing are best thickened by reduction or with cornflour, as flour-thickened sauces are likely to curdle when reheated. Only mayonnaise and custard sauces cannot be frozen, since the ingredients freeze at different temperatures and give unsatisfactory results.

Sauces can be stored in large quantities in cartons, or in 'brick' form using loaf tins. Small quantities can be frozen in ice cube trays, then wrapped individually in foil and packed in quantities in bags for easy storage.

Flans (Savoury and Sweet)

Preparation   Prepare and bake flan, and finish completely. Freeze on a tray without wrappings. Wrap in foil or polythene, or pack in box to prevent damage.

Serving   Thaw in loose wrappings at room temperature for 2 hours. Reheat if required.
High Quality Storage Life   2 months (fresh filling); 1 month (leftover meat or vegetables)

Some savoury and sweet flans suitable for the freezer.

Pasta

Preparation Slightly undercook macaroni, spaghetti or other pasta. Drain thoroughly and cool. Pack in polythene bags in usable quantities.

Serving Plunge into boiling water. Bring water to the boil and cook pasta until just tender.
High Quality Storage Life 1 month

Rice

Preparation Slightly undercook rice. Drain thoroughly and pack in polythene bags in usable quantities.

Serving (a) Plunge into boiling water. Bring water to boil and cook rice until just tender. (b) Reheat in melted butter in a thick pan. (c) Reheat in a shallow pan in a low oven.
High Quality Storage Life 1 month

FREEZING PUDDINGS

Preparation for Freezing of Puddings

A wide variety of puddings can be frozen and are useful for emergency use; this can also be a way of storing surplus fruit in a convenient form. Puddings which can be frozen include obvious items such as ice cream and pies, and pancakes and sponge-cakes which can be combined quickly with fruit, cream or sauces to make complete puddings. Steamed puddings can also be frozen, together with fruit crumbles, gelatine sweets, cold soufflés and mousses and cheesecakes. Milk puddings do not freeze well, however, since they become mushy or curdle.

Baked and Steamed Puddings

These can be made from almost all standard cake and pudding recipes, and are most easily made in foil containers which can be used for freezing and for heating. It is better not to put jam or syrup in the bottom of these puddings before cooking, as they become soggy on thawing, but dried fruit, fresh fruits and nuts can be added. Highly-spiced puddings may develop off-flavours.

Suet puddings containing fresh fruit can be frozen raw or cooked. It is more useful, however, to cook them before freezing, since only a short time need then be allowed for reheating before serving. Puddings made from cake mixtures, or any traditional sponge or suet puddings, can also be frozen raw or cooked. Cake mixtures can be used to top such fruits as apples, plums, gooseberries and apricots; these are just as easily frozen raw since the complete cooking time in the oven is only a little longer than reheating time. This also applies to fruit puddings with a crumble topping.

156

A steamed pudding packed in a foil container for freezing, and reheated in the same container two months later.

Fruit Puddings

It is useful to use some fruit to make prepared puddings for the freezer. Fruit in syrup can be flavoured with wine or liqueurs and needs no further cooking; this is particularly useful for such fruits as pears and peaches which are difficult to freeze well in their raw state.

Gelatine Puddings

Many cold puddings involve the use of gelatine. When gelatine is frozen in a creamy mixture, it is entirely successful, although clear jellies are not recommended for the freezer. The ice crystals formed in freezing break up the structure of the jelly, and while it retains its setting quality, the jelly becomes granular and uneven and loses clarity. This granular effect is masked in such puddings as mousses.

Pudding Sauces

A supply of sweet sauces such as fruit sauce or chocolate sauce can be usefully frozen for use with puddings or ices. These are best prepared and frozen in small containers, and reheated in a double boiler.

Mousses and Cold Soufflés

Preparation   Prepare in serving dishes if these are freezer-tested.

Serving   Thaw in refrigerator for 8 hours.
High Quality Storage Life   1 month

Steamed and Baked Puddings

Preparation   Prepare standard sponge pudding or cake mixture recipes. Use with jam, fresh or dried fruit. Steam or bake in foil containers. Cool completely. Cover with foil or pack in polythene bag.

Serving   Thaw at room temperature for 2 hours. Steam for 45 minutes.
High Quality Storage Life   4 months

157

FREEZING SNACKS AND APPETISERS

Appetisers

Preparation   Wrap rindless bacon round chicken livers, cocktail sausages, seafood or cooked prunes. Secure with cocktail sticks. Fast-freeze on trays. Transfer to polythene bags for storage.

Serving   Cook frozen appetisers under grill or in hot oven until bacon is crisp.
High Quality Storage Life   2 weeks

Canapés

Preparation   Cut day-old bread into shapes, but do not use toast or fried bread. Spread butter to edge of bread. Add toppings, but avoid hard-boiled egg whites or mayonnaise. Aspic becomes cloudy on thawing. Fast-freeze unwrapped on trays. Pack in boxes for storage.

Serving   Thaw on dish 1 hour before serving. Garnish if necessary.
High Quality Storage Life   2 weeks

Dips

Preparation   Make dips with a base of cottage or cream cheese. Avoid mayonnaise, hard-boiled egg whites or crisp vegetables. Pack in waxed or rigid plastic containers. Overwrap if dips contain garlic or onion.

Serving   Thaw in containers at room temperature for 5 hours. Blend in mayonnaise, egg whites or vegetables if necessary.
High Quality Storage Life   1 month

Flavoured Butters

Preparation   (a) Fast-freeze butter balls or curls on trays. Transfer to polythene bags for storage. (b) Cream butter with herbs, lemon juice, or shellfish. Form into cylinders and wrap in greaseproof paper and polythene.

Serving   (a) Thaw in serving dishes at room temperature for 1 hour. (b) Cut in slices to put on hot meat or fish.
High Quality Storage Life   6 months (unsalted); 3 months (salted)

INDEX